© 1995 BY JULIE METZ

LONE JENSEN experienced three visitations from Mary that inspired her to seek out other people with similar encounters who, like her, continue to feel Mary's presence and power infusing their daily lives. She was born in Køge, Denmark, and now lives in Sparta, New Jersey.

GIFTS OF GRACE

GIFTS
OF
GRACE

*A Gathering of Personal Encounters
with the Virgin Mary*

LONE JENSEN

rayo
An Imprint of HarperCollinsPublishers

FIRST RAYO EDITION PUBLISHED 2004.

Designed by Laura Lindgren

The Library of Congress has catalogued the hardcover edition as follows:

Jensen, Lone.
    Gifts of Grace : a gathering of personal encounters with the Virgin Mary / Lone Jensen. — 1st ed.
        p.   cm.
    ISBN 0-06-017351-3
    1. Mary, Blessed Virgin, Saint—Apparitions and miracles.
I. Title.
BT650.J46   1995
232.91´7—dc20   95-4962

ISBN 0-06-056695-7 (pbk.)

04 05 06 07 08 OS/RRD 10 9 8 7 6 5 4 3 2 1

In grateful appreciation to everyone who so generously shared with me their encounters and experiences with the Virgin Mary. May our stories assure others that we are not alone, and that there is truly a Divine Mother for us all.

CONTENTS

Do not be troubled or weighed down with grief.
Do not fear any illness or vexation, anxiety or pain.
Am I not here who am your Mother?
Are you not under my shadow and protection?
Am I not your fountain of life?
Are you not in the folds of my mantle?
In the crossing of my arms?
Is there anything else you need?

THE VIRGIN MARY
TO JUAN DIEGO IN 1531

INTRODUCTION

THROUGHOUT the world today, there is an interest in the redemptive quality of spirituality. This powerful awakening is communicating itself in many ways, from the beguiling goodness of angels, revelations on death and dying that we have learned about through the sharing of near-death experiences, to the popularity of works like *A Course in Miracles*, and more. There has been a resurrection of love in our society, a return to the feminine strengths of nurturing, caring, and compassion. Who better than the Virgin Mary to lead us on this journey back to God?

The Virgin Mary is the embodiment of Motherhood. Her appearances to so many people of varied faiths have signaled a time of peace and hope, a return to the love of God. Long after her earthly role as the Mother of Christ was fulfilled, Mary's presence has been with us, and in the last two thousand years every continent has been witness to her apparitional return. Perhaps we should take a quick look back in order to understand how we have arrived at an age that is being showered with her graces.

*　　*　　*

When the Angel Gabriel appeared to the Virgin and proclaimed her Handmaiden of the Lord, the simple life of a young girl was forever transformed. She became an integral part of an epic that continues to unfold today. Her role has scarcely changed over time, but the mantle that once covered the Christ child has now enveloped the world, blanketing us in her loving embrace. This love—regardless of race, color, or creed, makes Mary a Universal Mother.

There are more than one hundred accounts of the Blessed Mother's return to earth before the 1900s, the most famous being at Lourdes, in France. A young girl there by the name of Bernadette Soubirous was visited in 1858 by the Virgin Mary, in a grotto that has since been the source of healings and spiritual awakenings for thousands of pilgrims from around the world. Bernadette was canonized. The film *The Song of Bernadette* is a modern testament to the miraculous events that have taken place there over time.

Almost equally well known are the events in Fatima, Portugal. In the spring of 1916 St. Michael, the Angel of Peace, appeared three times to three young children before announcing that Our Lady would soon come. She came on May 13, 1917, and asked the children to meet her in a sheep pasture on the outskirts of the village on the thirteenth of every month thereafter. She promised them that if Russia was consecrated to her, the world would enjoy a period of great peace and harmony. Unfortunately this did not happen, and the world soon witnessed two monstrous world wars.

Mary also promised a miracle at twelve noon on October 13, 1917. By the time October arrived, word had spread throughout Europe and seventy thousand people had crowded into the sheep pasture in anticipation. They were drenched in a deluge of rain, but then a great solar phenomenon appeared: the sun, exploding like a ball of fire, plunged toward the earth. After twelve long minutes, it reverted to its normal position, leaving the mud soaked ground and the clothing of the witnesses instantaneously dry—and then the Virgin appeared. The story of the miracle is still the source of much speculation in spiritual circles.

I was not one of the people who would have heard about Lourdes or Fatima, or any other miracle for that matter. I was born in Køge, Denmark, a city just outside of Copenhagen, to a family that categorically denied the existence of anything beyond the physical or scientific realms. It wasn't only that we didn't practice any form of organized religion, it was that we simply did not believe. We did not speak of God. We never went to a worship service of any kind. And we certainly never prayed. This lack of spiritual conviction was not the result of being fiercely intellectual, or academic, or scientific. I can't say that it was simply because we were Danish either, although Denmark is not noted for its spiritual devotion. My parents, and theirs before them, just did not believe in a higher power.

Our lack of devotion did not prevent me from having a happy childhood, and I never really felt that I was missing anything. When I was still quite young, we moved to the United States, and I was faced with learning a new language. This move engendered a curiosity about people of different worlds, and different beliefs, that was instrumental in the direction my life has taken.

My third grade teacher used to spend his summers teaching school children in Kenya. He brought back the names of a few children and we were asked to correspond with them as part of a school project. I picked a boy and began a friendship that would last for the next twelve years. Our correspondence was particularly meaningful to me because of my father. He had not been present at my birth; he had been in Africa, an executive of a company that sought to mine the rich mineral deposits off the coast of Angola. My pen pal, too, was a key influence in the development of my interest in foreign cultures and their languages.

When I was in seventh grade, I took a course in the introduction of foreign languages. I studied German, Spanish, Russian, and—my favorite— French. It was French that led me to an experience I would later look back upon as a significant turning point in my life.

At fifteen, I became one of a handful of American students admitted to a small boarding school in the French Alps. I lived in Evian-les-Bains, and, along with a girlfriend who shared my insatiable curiosity, spent every weekend traveling by train to enchanting French towns and villages. We were so adventurous, and believed that anything was pos-

sible—which certainly proved to b
Paris.

We were there for two weeks of exp.
one day we came upon the Cathédral de N
de Paris at dusk. It is impossible to describe t.
nificent presence of this building, especially .
fading light. The church is architecturally formid.
and simply breathtaking. The moment I entered th
arched doorways, my senses reeled. White candles
flickered everywhere; there was a rich scent of rose
incense in the air; the dying daylight drifted through
the incredible stained-glass windows, casting soft
rainbows of color inside the stone structure. What
struck me most were the images of the Madonna. She
was so beautiful and seemed to look down upon me
with a tenderness and compassion that I had never
known. Everything about her, from the gentle tilt of
her head to her outstretched arms seemed to say:
"Thank you for coming in to see me . . . I have been
waiting for you . . . and I love you." This place was so
intensely quiet, so reverent. I remember thinking
suddenly, "Oh my God, this is religious!"

I should say that throughout my childhood, I
always felt particularly protected and very, very
lucky. It was as if I believed that no harm would
come to me. I felt a force of grace surrounding me.
I just thought that everybody had this same feeling,
but I did not know that it was considered spiritual
in nature. That is why I was so overwhelmed at
Notre Dame. It was the first time in my life that I
equated those feelings with God! And it was the

first time I felt that I was actually a spiritual person.

After this, I spent much time traveling throughout Europe exploring medieval chateaux and cathedrals. I was so curious about how people lived then and I wanted to know what force had inspired them to build these monumental Houses of God. This became a very mystical time in my life. Yet when I returned to the United States, I moved on.

I continued to study other cultures as a foreign language major in college. I took French, as well as Japanese and Russian, and I especially loved looking for the similarities between diverse cultures. I found a job as a marketing apprentice with an international hospitality firm in my junior year. They later hired me as a full time writer of press materials. This firm represented properties in Tokyo, Scotland, Australia, and we were just beginning to construct a small luxury hotel in Santa Fe, New Mexico.

Being in Santa Fe—literally the City of Holy Faith—is like taking a walk back in time. It is a land of stark contrasts, and the spirit of the diverse communities is very engaging, especially since the Native Americans and Hispanics far outnumber the Anglos. Despite a history of violent conflict, the Native and Hispanic communities share a devotion to Mary as Our Lady of Guadalupe! She is everywhere in Santa Fe: painted on adobe walls, smiling from bumper stickers, riding on the dashboards of cars. She is invoked, praised, and celebrated in special processions and religious services throughout the year, and the oldest extant shrine in the United States is in Santa Fe—the Santuario de Guadalupe.

I was mesmerized by people's devotion to this Madonna throughout my stay in this special city, but one incident stands out. I was at a small dinner party when a Native American elder brought out a photograph he wanted to share with the rest of us. He explained that he had been driving between New Mexico and Colorado when he heard a woman's voice calling him. He pulled over to the side of the road, and then walked to the edge of a canyon that had been a sacred place to the Pueblo Indians for hundreds of years. He called Mary the Blue Lady and told us that when he was standing at the edge of the canyon, she had appeared to him in a hovering thirty-foot, ethereal apparition. She was bathed in blue light, her hands folded in prayer. He wouldn't tell us what she said, but that he had asked her if he could take a picture with the camera he had in his car. She said yes, and that miraculous image was the photo I held in my hand! He also had a photograph of the Madonna cradling the Christ child, taken by a sixty-eight-year-old widow in Queensland, Australia, in 1982, as well as a third picture, of Mary's face emerging from the clouds.

I was amazed by this tangible confirmation of Mary's presence in our world. I started to think about my own experience with Mary in Notre Dame and wondered why I had been so touched by her there. It slowly dawned on me that she had probably always been with me, gifting me with her graces and that sense of protection that I had felt. I was inspired to learn more.

I discovered that Our Lady of Guadalupe had first appeared to an Indian, Juan Diego, on December 9, 1531, in a place called Tepeyac Hill. He heard music and, out of curiosity, climbed the hill to find a lady of great beauty and brilliance. She greeted him and said, "Juanito, my son, dearest of my sons, I am your merciful Mother, the Mother of all who live united in this land, and of all mankind, of all those who love me, of those who cry to me, of those who confide in me." She appeared for four consecutive days and asked Juan Diego to have the bishop build a temple for her on Tepeyac Hill. Bishop Zumarraga doubted the divine origin of the request, and demanded the Lady produce a sign that she was really from heaven.

On the third day, Juan's uncle fell ill with cocolixtle, a dreaded and usually fatal disease. Juan tried to avoid the Lady that day, thinking that he was too busy to talk to her. Mary found him running around the other side of the hill and asked him why he was in such a hurry. He explained that his uncle was dying, but she assured him that she had already cured him. She then told him to go to the top of Tepeyac Hill and gather the flowers he would find there. Since it was December, Juan was startled to see a patch of Castillian roses in bloom, when he expected nothing but thistles and cacti. Using his *tilma*—a type of overcloth—as an apron, he gathered the roses, and returned to find the Lady waiting. She rearranged the flowers in the *tilma* and asked him to go straight to the bishop without letting anyone see what he was carrying. When he was finally granted an audience with Bishop Zumarraga, Juan Diego released the cloth, spilling forth the roses. To his amazement, the *tilma* miraculously bore the exact image of the Lady that Juan Diego had seen!

The *tilma* exists intact to this day, housed in the Basilica in Mexico City. It is made of ayate fibers from the maguey cactus, which produces a coarse fabric. The normal life span of such a cloth is twenty years unpainted, and approximately six years painted, yet 464 years later, the image remains. It is the only time in recorded history that Mary left an image of herself.

Modern scientific methods have authenticated the miraculous nature of the picture, and no art authority in the world has been able to explain why there are no brush strokes or cracking, which would be characteristic of aged paint. Fifty-nine years ago, Richard Kuhn, a Nobel Prize–winning chemist from Germany, declared that when the fibers of the cloth were examined individually, they contained no coloring of any kind. In other words, the colors used to create the image were not derived from any known animal, vegetable, or mineral dyes in the world.

Our Lady of Guadalupe appeared to an Indian man, called for a place of worship on Indian soil, and spoke the local Indian language. She manifested herself as an Indian Queen, the blue-green color of her robes being the exact same color as the robes worn by Aztec royalty in that age. It has always fascinated me that there is such a mix of Aztec and Christian symbols on the *tilma*, as if Mary was trying to unite the two cultures and end the bloody strife that had torn them apart for so long—a message that she has continued to bring to other lands in later times.

There are so many inexplicable details in the miraculous *tilma* that it must be recognized as a truly remarkable work of divine art. It is as if Mary knows our need for tangible signs, and has given us this cloth as an enduring example of the reality of her presence amongst us.

In our more recent past, Mary has come to a small mountain village known as Garabandal. Like Tepeyac Hill and other apparition sites, Garabandal is a quiet place largely untouched by modern life. It is interesting to me that Mary's appearances here coincided with the Cuban missile crisis—a time when our world was plagued by confusion and in the midst of enormous change.

An angel appeared to four young girls in Garabandal on the evening of June 18, 1961. Conchita Gonzales, Maria Dolores Mazon, Jacinta Gonzales, and Maria Cruz Gonzales were eleven and twelve years old, and together they came to be visited by the angel eight times in the next twelve days. On July 2, Mary revealed herself to the girls with two angels by her side. That was the first of more than two thousand apparitions that took place in Garabandal between 1961 and 1965.

The young girls always knew when Mary would be appearing because they felt what they called the three joys: the first was a slight feeling, then a more intense sensation, and finally a strong interior calling that would lead them to meet Mary wherever she was appearing. Even though each of the girls would come from a different part of the village, they always arrived to see her at exactly the same time.

The girls all described Mary in the same way: they said her deep nut-brown hair was waist length, and she wore it parted in the center. Her features were delicate, her hands slender, and she called herself Our Lady of Carmel. Although she spoke to them in a voice from heaven, they said that she wanted them to speak to her as if she were their earthly Mother. She wanted to know everything they were thinking and feeling. These conversations were often accompanied by many unexplained phenomena that defied natural law. I have seen black and white film footage of the children levitating up to kiss their spiritual Mother. They were also photographed in ecstatic falls, where their bodies were molded into sculptural positions—and not even four doctors could budge them. They were seen walking forward and backward over very difficult, rocky ground, with their heads tilted straight back and their eyes looking up toward heaven. Before the final apparition, Mary said to Conchita, "I did not come just for the people of Garabandal, but rather for the whole world, for all of mankind." This is one of the messages that Mary repeats with increasing frequency to the children of the world.

There are other apparition sites that have touched me deeply. One is in Betania, Venezuela, where

Maria Esperanza Bianchini, a mother of five, has been seeing the Virgin. She had been seeing Mary and other saints since childhood, but on March 25, 1984, the Virgin Mary made her presence known to everyone. Calling herself the Reconciler of Nations and People, she would appear suddenly and stay usually ten to fifteen minutes at a time. Thousands of people have made pilgrimages to Betania, and many of them have seen her bathed in light. They see her as a three-dimensional being, wearing blue, and they often smell a strong scent of roses. Maria has said that the time for people to awaken spiritually has come, and that these apparitions from their Mother are a call to all human beings for reconciliation.

Similarly, on June 30, 1985, Mary appeared to Julia Kim in Naju, Korea. This time she called herself the Mediatrix of All Nations, and asked for us to pray and turn our struggles into graces.

On April 26, 1987—the exact anniversary date and at the exact hour of the Chernobyl disaster—Mary appeared in the Soviet Ukraine, this time promising peace. Thousands came from the farthest reaches of Russia to see her. People of all faiths and traditions were there, and Lutherans, Muslims, and Jews all saw her. I understand that she continues to bless the people there by appearing in open fields and at shrines throughout the Ukraine.

The visionaries and the countries may change, but Mary's message remains the same: peace, prayer, and turning our hearts to God. She urges us to pray so that the peace of God may descend and envelop us all.

There have actually been more than three hundred apparitions reported since the dawning of the twentieth century, with a marked increase in the frequency of her visits as we approach the millennium. Italy, Brazil, Germany, Belgium, Holland, Sweden, Switzerland, France, Bolivia, Ecuador, Venezuela, Argentina, Costa Rica, Guatemala, Chile, Czechoslovakia, Turkey, Israel, Poland, Egypt, Japan, Syria, Lebanon, China, Korea, Kenya, India, the Soviet Ukraine, and the United States have all hosted the Divine Mother.

Perhaps the best known site today is Medjugorje, a remote mountain village in the Province of Bosnia-Herzegovina. Since June 24, 1981, Mary has been appearing daily to six children, calling herself the Queen of Peace. More than fifteen million people have made a pilgrimage to this tiny village and many continue to go. It is the longest, most public series of continuous visits in the world. Mary has told one of her visionaries, Vicka Ivankovich, that her messages are for everyone equally, regardless of race or religion. She said that it was not God who separated people, since there is no division in heaven, but people who divide themselves.

Mary wants us to pray for global peace. In one of her messages she says, "My dear, dear children, the world has forgotten the value of prayer and fasting. With prayer and fasting, wars could be stopped and natural laws suspended." This message was given in precisely the same area that would later become ravaged by war. Mary must have known what was going to happen there and began to urge people to pray years before the conflict erupted.

A similar incident occurred in Kibeho, Rwanda. Known as the Mother of the Word, Mary started appearing to seven young people in November of 1991: Anathalie Mukamazimpaka, Marie-Claire Mukangango, Stephanie Mukamurenzi, Agnes Kamagaju, Alphonsine Mumureke, Emmanuel Segastashya, and Vestine Salima are the visionaries who reported that Mary was once again calling our attention to the importance of prayer as a path to peace—years before the area exploded in civil war.

There is a popular belief that Mary and Joseph passed through Zeitun, Egypt, as they fled from Herod's persecution. I wonder about the coincidence of Mary's return to Zeitun right before the first peace treaty was signed in the Middle East. She was spotted on April 2, 1968, on the top of Saint Mary's Coptic Icon Church, moving along the domes. She came as often as two or three times a week and her visits lasted from a few minutes, up to eight hours. During the two years of her apparitions, the crowds grew and millions of people from all races, classes, occupations, and religions saw her. Everyone present could see her surrounded by a luminous white light, or sometimes in a multitude of colors. She often carried an olive branch and blessed the people below. Many miraculous healings were reported, but no one received any particular messages from the Virgin. Her presence alone was enough to touch the hearts of the Orthodox,

Catholic, Protestant, Jewish, and Muslim people who came to visit with her.

Nostradamus, which means "Our Lady" in Latin, was one of her devotees. It is certainly conceivable that she is the one who imparted to him the faculty of divining the future as a way of passing on her warnings to humanity.

With the passage of time, Mary's messages have moved from predictions of widespread destruction and calamity, such as Nostradamus foretold, to promises of global peace, hope, and love. She herself even seems to be appearing differently. She once wore only the color blue that we have come to associate with her, but has now been seen in the softest pink with gold finery. It is a nurturing, feminine color, a color of love and gentle compassion, that reflects the new emphasis in her messages.

Mary has always been known as the Queen of Angels, and the recent explosion of interest in these beings of light strikes me. Angels have always come to announce her apparitions, and they often escort her from heaven. I wonder if the angels haven't come again today to herald a widespread recognition of the Divine Mother. We desperately need her loving guidance at this time, and she is here to return us to a state of joy.

I had my own experience with an angel at an apparition site in Colorado. I arrived early at the Mother Cabrini Shrine. I had a few hours to wait in the cold before the apparition was to take place and was wondering how to pass the time. All of a sudden, I felt a rush of heat. I looked up and a ball of pale green light was floating about ten or twelve feet from me. It was three feet in diameter and it moved very deliberately, as it slowly took on the form of an angel. It reminded me of a butterfly emerging from a cocoon, as the wings took shape first, followed by the body. I believe that I was seeing the Angel Gabriel. Although he didn't speak to me, his presence did indeed herald Mary's manifestations in my own life.

Shortly thereafter, I began to sense Mary with me often. I would smell the distinct scent of roses when I thought of her—and I also began to see her in my dreams.

As I became more and more involved in spiritual studies, I wanted a career that would support my spiritual life. I resigned from my job with the hospitality firm, not knowing exactly which direction my life would take.

At the time, I was in the habit of taking long walks in the morning. One gloriously beautiful day, as I moved along a particular dirt road in Santa Fe, something very special happened. The New Mexico sun bathed the land in a golden yellow light. I came to a fork in the road and that is when I saw the sparkles up ahead, glistening in the air. As I walked toward them, Mary appeared directly in front of me. Her hair was soft brown and her heart-shaped face was so angelic. She wore all white, with gold ties at her waist and gold trim running along the hem of her gown. She never spoke, but she stretched out her arms to me and that is when I knew with certainty that I was right in pursuing a new direction in my life. She confirmed for me that she was truly calling me down a different road and that she would be there to guide me.

As the next few years went by, I met others who shared my interest and affection for Mary. The meetings always seemed to be chance encounters in bookshops or restaurants, in grocery stores or standing in line at the post office. The stories of her at work, blessing the world, really moved me. My friends loved hearing them as well and it was the recognition of how much we enjoyed sharing these Marian encounters that became the inspiration for this book.

Everything I have learned about Mary, and all that I have come to believe about her purpose in returning to earth over and over again, is demonstrated in the stories you are about to read.

Mary consoles the whole spectrum of the human experience. She visits us. She heals us. She helps us to grow in our relationships. She strengthens us in the face of death and promises eternal life to the dying. She nurtures our faith, and our lives are never again the same after she touches our hearts. These are the five parts of the book, and I am deeply grateful to Mary for bringing all of these people whose stories make up these parts into my life. I truly appreciate their willingness to share. Every one of them was introduced to me in a special way, or came to me by word of mouth, eager to speak about their experiences with Mary. I believe that this book has happened because she wants us to see how she can help.

She is here for all people of every race and religion. She is here to reconcile our differences and to unite us in our collective return to God. She is here to touch our hearts so that we can be open to the power of love.

Centuries ago, only a few exalted people were blessed by the Divine Mother. Saints encountered her and we were awed by their mystical experiences that seemed so removed from our ordinary lives.

Mary has always been with us and she wants us to know that there is no need that is too small or too great for her attention. She thinks of us all as her children, and wants to heal our hurts and vanquish our fears. She has come with a message of peace and unity. She promises to return us to spiritual wholeness when we open our hearts to God, through prayer. She is the embodiment of love and compassion, and an encounter with the Virgin Mary leaves no one unaffected.

Truly, her presence amongst us is a gift of grace.

LONE JENSEN
Sparta, New Jersey

VISITATIONS

*A maid of fourteen rose to my sight like a full
moon. She was exalted in majesty above time
and transcended it in pride and glory. . . . Thou
art a pyx containing blended odours and per-
fume, thou art a meadow producing spring-
herbs and flowers. Beauty reached in thee her
utmost limit: another like thee is impossible.*

IBN´ ARABI

JN LATE 1991, our son Jimmy was four years old.
He was a very special child for my husband, Jim,
and me, having survived a difficult premature
birth. He was born two and a half months early,
weighing only two and a half pounds. It was a real
struggle for him to be here.

In early November of that year, I heard about a
woman by the name of Theresa Lopez. She was
supposedly hearing from the Blessed Mother Mary,
who was appearing to her monthly at the Mother
Cabrini Shrine just west of Denver, Colorado. Hundreds, even thousands, of people were congregating
there every month for the apparitions. I wasn't

really sure whether I believed that the Blessed Mother could be seen, but I was curious. The next time the Blessed Mother was supposed to appear was November 10, and so I decided to ask Jim if he would like to take a drive to the shrine after our eleven o'clock mass at our church here in Colorado Springs. He agreed, and off we went with Jimmy.

We didn't arrive at the shrine until three o'clock and Jimmy had fallen asleep in the backseat. We were supposed to meet relatives, so Jim and I decided to let Jimmy sleep while we went looking for them. As we walked around, a woman pointed out the visionary, Theresa Lopez, and I went over to introduce myself. She spoke briefly to me about Mary's appearance to her earlier in the day, but I remained skeptical. It was so hard to believe that someone had actually spoken to the Blessed Mother!

Even though we had missed the apparition, we did want to say a prayer at the shrine, so we went back to the car to wake Jimmy. As we climbed the steep steps leading up to the Cabrini Shrine, Jimmy was having a good time playing around with his cousins, not really paying much attention to the adults or to what we were doing. When we reached the top, we all recognized the dirt hill area where it was said Theresa saw Our Lady. We saw that someone had placed a rose in a dry bush nearby. We said our prayer. Then we sang a song to her, and a few other people standing around joined us. When we finished, it became completely silent. Even the children were silent. People were meditating and praying, and I knelt down to hug my son, asking the Blessed Mother to pray for him. As I stood up, Jimmy took my hand and, since he had recently started to wear thick eyeglasses, I said, "Ask Mary to help your eyes heal, Jimmy."

We resumed talking and everyone was enjoying our visit together, while Jimmy went down to the fence. He stood there for a minute or two, looking up into the sky, and then he ran back to me. He tugged at my leg and asked, "Can you see her?" I was in the middle of talking to my mom and he kept interrupting me, saying, "Can you see her?" I finally stopped and asked, "See who?" "It's the Blessed Mother! Can't you see her? She's right there—sparkling!"

I was in a state of disbelief. I did not know what to think. I asked him to describe what he was seeing. "She's changing colors," he began, "but she's very pink. She has sparkles on top of her head, and her hair is brown. And she's wearing a towel on her head. She's standing on something brown, and there are stars under her feet. I see a lot of colors around her—pink, red, white, blue."

I said that if the Blessed Mother is really there, we should say a prayer. Jimmy took my hand and we went down to the chain-link fence. Two of his cousins followed and we knelt down beside Jimmy. Then I said, "Help us to be good and follow in the footsteps of your Son, Jesus Christ." It was not a formal prayer, but words that came spontaneously, from my heart. When I finished, Jimmy said, "Did you hear her?" "No," I told him. "What did she say?" "She said, 'I will.'"

I was overwhelmed. There were people behind us and I could see that their eyes were filled with tears, and I realized they had heard what Jimmy had said. I really was numb, even as my own tears started to flow. This was a very special moment for us all, but later, when some of the emotion of the experience had abated, we found ourselves questioning whether or not Jimmy could have made it up. At one point afterward he told my sister Annette that the Blessed Mother looked like his mommy! Could a child's overactive imagination have been at work?

I have gone over it in my mind many, many times, and I really don't think he could have made something like that up on the spur of the moment. He had been asleep in the car when Theresa was speaking to us, so he couldn't have heard what she said. And on the way up the hill to the shrine, he was fooling around with his cousins, walking ahead of us so he wasn't near anyone who could have told him anything about how Mary had looked when she appeared to Theresa.

Two days later I attended a prayer meeting in Colorado Springs and Theresa was there, describing what she had seen when Mary had appeared to her. "She was dressed all in pink, with a gold tie around her waist," she said. "And she wore a gold crown with hundreds of sparkling points and stood on a pedestal of light." I began to weep because that was exactly what my son had seen! I had no more doubt, no more skepticism.

A week later, on that Wednesday, which was the feast day of St. Francis Xavier Cabrini, we returned to the shrine. Jimmy and I drove up from Colorado Springs with my parents and my in-laws. He was sitting in the front with my parents, and as we were driving, my mother noticed that he was staring out the window, smiling. When she asked him what he was looking at and why he was smiling, he said that he was looking at the Blessed Mother. "I think she's following me," he said. "She's smiling at me."

When we arrived at the Cabrini Shrine, Jimmy could still see Our Lady and the colors. I kept asking him all kinds of questions, but he would just say, "Mom, I already told you. I see the same as last time!" And then he did the sweetest thing. He handed me his eyeglasses and said, "Here, put these on. Maybe you'll see her."

There has been no miracle of restored vision for my son, but he certainly "sees" more than my husband and I. Jimmy has now seen and described "the colors" three or four times, and in our home. He consistently sees the same colors: pink, red, white, and blue. He tries to jump up and touch them, that's how real they are to him. He says the colors make him happy, that Jesus sent them down from heaven with his Mother and that they kind of look like a rainbow. He makes a swirling motion with his hand to describe how they disappear. As he puts it, they "make like a design and poke a hole and go up to heaven."

This doesn't happen with Jimmy at our request or prompting when he wants something. Usually, he likes for either his father or me to lie in bed with him until he goes to sleep, making excuses like "I have bad dreams" or "I don't feel good." But when he sees the colors, he says they make him feel good and happy—and he isn't afraid.

But it doesn't happen at will.

One day he asked me if I knew about "the story that fell from the colors on the mountain with all the stars." I didn't really know what he meant, but I did know my son couldn't read yet. He asked me if I knew why Jesus had died. I wanted him to tell me and he answered, "He died for us, so we could be with him in heaven some day."

On more than one occasion, Jimmy has begun to cry, saying that he doesn't want us to go to heaven yet, that he wants us to stay home with him. We've tried to explain that there's no need for him to be afraid or to worry about that, because God will take care of us. I'm not sure we've convinced him though, since he still will talk about us going to heaven soon.

Jimmy's encounters with the Blessed Mother have not changed our lives except in the most fundamental and important way. Our son's experiences have brought the whole family a deepening of our faith. We have always believed in the importance and the power of prayer, but our son has helped us "see" more clearly than before. I hope that sharing his experience will do the same for others.

JIMMY, JIM, AND MICHELLE LOBATO
Colorado Springs, Colorado

I WAS ONLY five when I had what was to be the first mystical experience of my life—only at the time I didn't know it was the first and I didn't find it mystical, but frightening! I was getting ready to go to bed for the night when I happened to look over at the window. I distinctly remember seeing an unmistakable silhouette of the Virgin Mary appear at that window. Although the image stayed for only a minute, and although I heard nothing, what I saw was very well defined, and it left a lasting impression. I knew that what had occurred was extremely unusual, something that didn't happen every day. At that age, it is awful to be singled out, so I kept the incident to myself and told no one about it.

Then when I was about six and a half years old, Castro had already taken power, and one of his decrees was the closing of anything Catholic. He ordered all the nuns and priests off the island, closed all churches, convents, and parochial schools. We lived close to a church, a convent, and a school, and reports began to circulate that one of the nuns who had lived and died at that convent was appearing on a balcony there. Despite our proximity, my family had never seen her, yet so many people had witnessed her apparition that it became an almost ordinary occurrence. For months, people would gather at various locations in the surrounding area to watch for her at night.

My grandfather and I were in the habit of taking an after-dinner stroll. We would walk around our block every night. Finally, on this one evening, we saw what other people had been seeing. We looked up as those around us were, and there we saw on the steeple—standing directly on the cross—this totally clear white apparition. There was no color at all— just an incredible, translucent image of the nun standing with her hands folded in prayer. And then she began to rotate in a complete three-hundred-and-sixty-degree circle! It was not an impression of her moving—you could actually see her turning! The longer we stood there, the more people arrived; soon ten turned into a crowd of several hundred to watch this crystal-clear vision turn on the cross of our convent.

My grandfather had me run back to our house to tell the rest of the family. My grandmother, great-grandmother, and I sat on our porch, where the apparition was completely visible since we were only two houses away, and we began to pray. Some time later, Magda, a cousin who lived about a mile away, came over. We were inside the house when suddenly Magda called out, "Marie Carmen, come here! Come here quickly!"

I went over to where Magda was standing at the window to see the Virgin Mary hovering there! Unlike the nun, Mary was in full color. She stood only about four feet tall, and she was radiantly, breathtakingly beautiful! The best way to describe her is luminescent, as colors shimmered off her rainbow-colored robe and her halolike rays from the sun. She was holding a rosary, her hands folded in prayer. There was such a sweetness and beauty to her that it was almost too painful to see. I began to cry uncontrollably and so did Magda. We called for the adults, but none of them could see her.

And then the Virgin Mary spoke to me. Her message wasn't verbal, it was telepathic, but I heard it as clearly as if she had voiced the words in my ear. "Because you have seen me, much more will be expected of you."

The apparition of the Virgin Mary that my cousin and I witnessed lasted for about half an hour, then disappeared, although the nun on the cross of the steeple remained visible until dawn. Even though my family stayed up all night, watching the nun, no one saw the Virgin Mary outside the window of our home except for Magda and me.

Just as my experience when I was five years old frightened me, this one, moving as it was, left me quite disturbed. I felt as if I were strange, as if I didn't quite belong, and I was confused and bothered by this. Nevertheless, I felt drawn to Mary, close to her in a way I could never satisfactorily explain to myself.

Then, as I entered my teens and even later, I pulled away from established religion and began to study philosophy and Eastern thought. As I got older, and was married, the Virgin Mary and my childhood experiences with her were all but forgotten, but she had not forgotten me.

My husband, an Italian man, and I were visiting Rome. My husband had a very violent temper and we had a lot of problems in our marriage. I was absolutely terrified of him and was lying awake in a hotel room one night thinking about what I should do. Then it happened again! There in a corner of the hotel room I saw an apparition of the Virgin Mary. This time, she was not in color as she had been when I was six and a half. This was more like hearing her telepathic message because I could see *in*, I could feel *through*—this was an inner seeing, my soul opening and receiving.

She told me that she wanted to help with my situation, knowing how deeply troubled I was, but that she couldn't because I had turned away from her. She told me to start praying the rosary and then I could be close to her again. I had no idea what to do—despite being raised Catholic, I had never said the rosary in my entire adult life.

I learned, and quickly, and just as she had said to me, she did help again. My self-esteem and my self-confidence underwent powerful changes, enough for me to ultimately leave the man I married, of whom I had been deathly afraid. Once that step was taken, I was really ready to move on in my life. I started my own publishing business and I even wrote two spiritual books myself—both of which were dedicated to Mary. And I have been to Medjugorje. When I walked up that hill, I felt her presence so strongly, and I felt emotionally cleansed, as if I had been given a new, clean slate to mark my life.

I may never see or hear the Blessed Mother again, but she will always be in my heart, giving me courage and strength.

MARIE ATKINSON
Edison, New Jersey

FOR AS LONG AS I could remember, I considered myself a devout person, but I don't think I really ever understood the true meaning of Christmas until 1991. Actually, it was a little earlier than that, December 16, to be exact. That is the day God blessed me with an event that would forever change me, strengthening my faith and restoring my spirit—gifts of that season that last a lifetime.

It was early morning of December 16, 1991. I thought I was in a light sleep, that kind of half dreaming, half-awake place right before the alarm goes off. Suddenly, I sensed that there was someone else in my bedroom, a woman. I don't know how she got there, and strangely enough, I wasn't at all frightened by her presence. She was dressed in a long, brown robe of some undistinguished material with a hood that covered her head and face. Nevertheless, I had a strong feeling that she was very old, an ancient one.

I sat up in bed, wondering who she was.

She said nothing in response, and still I wasn't scared. Almost without even knowing I was doing it, I got out of bed and started to move toward her, drawn toward her as flowers are to the warmth and radiance of the sun.

Soon we were face-to-face, and I could see that she was smiling at me. It was the most exquisite smile I have ever looked upon, so filled with compassion and peace and understanding that I could feel my soul swelling from the beauty and serenity.

Slowly, she pushed back the hood, and all I could do was stare in amazement as the old woman became younger and younger, her face luminous, as if lighted from within by love. She was so incredibly beautiful and I could see then that it was the Virgin Mary! I simply knelt before her, so moved by her presence that it seemed the most natural thing for me to do. She then raised her arms heavenward, and cried out, "God's love for us is so great!"

As soon as she spoke those words, a dazzling light engulfed me. I had the most inexplicable impression that pure love was washing over me, filling me, making me better somehow. As strong as my faith had been up to then, I had not a clue, absolutely no idea whatsoever, about what was going on in my room that early morning or why. What I did know was that never in my life had I felt such freedom from fear; it was just a complete absence of an emotion that would have seemed quite natural under the circumstances, but it wasn't there, not at all.

She disappeared as silently and gently, and unexpectedly, as she had arrived. I wondered what, exactly, had happened in my room and thought maybe I had experienced a particularly potent and unusual dream, that you might say was mystical.

If the experience lingered within me, I wasn't really aware of it, as I raced around getting dressed, putting on my new suit and worrying about getting my daughter to school and myself to work. I did feel a stronger level of calm that was unique for me, but other than that, it was business as usual.

Well, maybe it wasn't business as usual, and maybe that feeling of calm was even stronger than I thought, and maybe that mystical dream had me more preoccupied than I imagined, because that very morning, as I was driving to work, I thought I was driving in my typically cautious, defensive way, especially by the big intersection near my office. But for some reason I misjudged when it was time to pull out into another lane. By the time I saw the huge, blue truck approaching, I had to swerve dangerously to avoid being hit and I crashed headlong into a telephone pole.

Over five hours of surgery. My body was a mess, but that was nothing compared to my face. My nose had been totally crushed. My cheekbones were fractured, my jaw broken. Everything would have to be reconstructed!

I spent three weeks recovering. I should have been hysterical during this time, worrying about what my face was going to look like. Amazingly, all that really occupied me during that time was why I had been saved from an accident that, by all accounts I had heard of the horrible wreckage, could have killed me. But I had lived, and I was getting better. Why? Why me? There had to be a reason.

Why had I been saved? I spent hours upon hours looking inward, thinking, questioning, wondering about my life and God's mysterious ways, and then I recalled that odd mystical dream I had had in the early morning of the day of my accident. I remembered the old woman turning young and lovely. I again saw myself kneeling before her. And that awesome light; how could I ever forget the sense of peace and goodness and love glowing from that light?

And so finally I had the answer to why I had been saved. The Blessed Mother had visited me that early morning to give me her strength and her love, and the wisdom of her words. That is what saw me through my ordeal. That is what allowed me to survive.

It took that experience for me to realize that my spirituality has to come first in my life. She was guiding me to that understanding, and she wants us to know that love is more important than anything! Love brings inner peace, peace in our families, and peace in our world. These are the things that God wants for us! Mary saved me not just with the gift of life, but with the gift of faith, and I hope I can do the same for others.

It is said that sometimes in life, accidents happen, but since that early morning of December 16, 1991, I know better!

MAUREEN COX
Dallas, Texas

ALTHOUGH I am not Catholic, I did go to Medjugorje in 1989. I went with three friends on a tour that included one priest and three nuns.

In Medjugorje, we found ourselves staying in the same house with a family who was related to the visionary Vicka, which proved very interesting. Mass is held at St. James Church every day, in four or five languages to accommodate the varied cultures of the people who go there. I did not go to confession as so many others did, but I went to talk to a priest who turned out to be a bit more narrow-minded than I would have hoped.

I believe very strongly that the Blessed Mother is a cosmic Mother, the Divine Mother who has come for all humanity. The priest could not understand this, and refused to call her divine. I explained that she's helping everyone on the planet, not just Catholics. We discussed philosophy and religion for three hours, and he just could not accept my beliefs.

When I finally left, he was dissatisfied that he had not converted me, and I was disappointed that his perspective was so limited.

That evening, in my room, I was about to tell two of my friends about the conversation with this priest when all of a sudden my heart started to flutter, and I said, "I feel we are going to be visited by the Blessed Mother now." I told my friends that we must be sitting up in a meditative position when she comes. My friends were greatly excited and we all got on the same bed to await the Divine Mother's arrival. With her came an energy, a radiance that was so bright, so strong, we couldn't even open our eyes!

I prayed to the Mother to let me see her with my naked eyes, and she did. I saw her floating in the air about two feet off the floor, close to the ceiling, because she is not very tall. Her gown was pink, the color of divine love that is shining on our planet now, and her veil was shimmering white. The first thing she said was that the priest I had spoken with that afternoon was her son and I should have patience with him. Then she brought the visionary Vicka into the room spiritually. The Blessed Mother talks to her every day, telling her the story of her life, and Vicka is to release that account as the Holy Mother guides her. She told me to listen to everything she has said to Vicka, and everything she will have to say. Then Vicka's spirit left the room.

The Divine Mother lifted her right hand, and pointed it at me and my friends, sending energy to our hearts. Then she spoke, and her message to us was: "I have come to open your hearts to receive all humanity." At that moment, my friends and I were holding hands tightly, our bodies shaking with the power of her energy. She just smiled at us with great understanding and love, then opened her arms really wide as if to receive us. Then she lowered her arms, went up through the ceiling, and disappeared.

I knew with a certainty after this that I am right in believing she is both cosmic and divine, a force of such love that she welcomes all faiths to her fold, and no one should ever think that they cannot reach out to her because she is here for us all.

MARIA
Los Angeles, California

I WAS BORN in America to parents of Italian descent, and all I can say about my life so far—and it's going on fifty years—is that being born into my extraordinary family gave me everything I needed for whatever life has dealt me.

I grew up in a family that was very religiously oriented, not so much in the sense of going to church regularly, but in having a really good personal relationship with God. And this began when my parents were both young and still living in

Italy. My mother has told me that when she was a child she would look out the window of her family's house and there before her was a clear vision of certain portions of her life yet to come. When those parts of her life arrived, she new exactly what was going to happen and so there was never any fear in her. My father, too, recalls a time when he was about twelve years old. He told me that he was just walking down the block as he often did, but for some reason this particular day he was filled with a feeling that he was special somehow—singled out, he thought. And just then white doves appeared in the sky above him, flying around him, and he understood instinctively that this was a sign for him, kind of like a promise that he had a special purpose here. I think he believed that that purpose was to pass on the strength of his faith, which both he and my mother have done.

I remember once when I was only about nine years old, and I was with two of my neighborhood friends. We were outside watching the sun set, and I remember it now as clearly as if it happened yesterday. Jesus appeared in the sky, and then the Sacred Heart. Even at nine years old, I had no doubt, no confusion about what I was seeing because of the faith my parents had imbued in me. As the vision faded, I turned to my friends, who said they had seen it too.

When I was thirteen, my grandfather passed away during the winter. In the spring, I saw him again—in a dream. I was in a bathroom-type of place, which I later interpreted to mean a place of spiritual cleansing, and my grandpa was standing right there. He didn't speak to me, which he never did when he was alive either, because he spoke only Italian, no English. In my dream, he pointed up toward what was an open sky, beckoning me to follow his pointing finger. And as I looked up I saw her, the Blessed Mother. The wind was blowing her dress, and around her head glittered the twelve stars. I felt her, felt that what I was seeing had to be real because of the way the wind blew around us and ruffled her beautiful blue mantle.

Then my grandpa brought down his hand, which had been closed, held his arm out to me, and opened his hand. There was the most exquisite gold medal with an image of the Madonna in an indescribable shade of blue! He placed the medal in my hand and tightened my fingers around it, and dream state or not, I *knew* I was really holding this wonderful medal of the Madonna! When I awoke the next morning, my fingers were curled over so tightly that when I finally opened my hand, I saw that I had left marks on my palm.

As the years progressed, and events occurred in my life that were difficult and trying, I turned with interest to study many world religions and spiritual traditions, wanting to learn about other mystical approaches to answering life's questions. It was when I was reading everything I could about palm-istry that I learned that between the love line and the heart line, on some people, what is known as a mystic cross may appear. Even though I read this years after the dream when I was thirteen, I at last understood what my grandpa had been telling me: that my life was under the protection of the Blessed Mother. And it has been! No matter what hardships or losses I have known, I believe absolutely that I have and always will have the protection of the Blessed Mother.

ROSEANN PROCOPIO
Lake Hopatcong, New Jersey

RAFAEL BLOM was a Croatian who left Yugoslavia before he finished his stint in the military, which was a requirement of all men. As a result, if he returned to his homeland he would be arrested immediately.

In 1981 when all the wonderful things began to happen in Medjugorje, Rafael felt compelled to do something for the Blessed Mother who was visiting his own country daily. He could not go back home to see her for himself, so he turned his California apartment into a place of prayer, doing everything he could to encourage devotion to the Blessed Mother and to spread her message. He even opened a bookstore in his apartment, selling spiritual books and a variety of devotional material. In addition, he had a large-screen television to show people his videos on spiritual subjects relating to the Virgin. Although his apartment was small, he would welcome fifty, sixty people at his prayer groups. All of us who attended and who knew Rafael miss him now that he has moved to Texas.

On Saturday, June 24, 1989, Rafael was having a special mass to celebrate the eighth anniversary of the Blessed Mother's apparitions in Medjugorje. He must have had about seventy-five people there, and I was one of the first to receive communion. It was quite extraordinary how I immediately felt the same kind of peace infuse me as I had experienced on visits I had made to Medjugorje. I knew instantly that Our Lady was with us that night.

As others received the host, I moved toward the balcony, looking out, but more absorbed in prayer than in observation. However, there seemed to be an oval-shaped opening in the trees directly in my line of vision, and we were on the third floor. I didn't pay much attention at first, but when I saw something move I stood riveted, watching carefully. I saw what was certainly Our Lady appearing a little smaller than life size and surrounded by a brilliant white light. She was dressed in a long white gown and held her arms outstretched.

Soon enough others came out on the balcony, exclaiming that they could see her, too. Some people burst into spontaneous hymns of praise and joy. I watched intently for about fifteen minutes, seeing her gently turn from side to side. A young boy of about eleven who was standing next to me said that she had a crown on her head and that she was standing on a platform between the trees, her arms held out.

I did not receive any specific message from her or inner locution, and to my knowledge no one else did either. The Blessed Mother's appearance in Pasadena, California, that night was similar to her visits in Ireland and in Russia, when she came just to make us aware that she is with us. She once told one of the visionaries that if it became necessary, she would go door to door to bring her children back to God. What better Mother could we have than one so filled with love for us, her children!

That special evening, which lasted from late afternoon until about eleven thirty at night, was extraordinary, but it wasn't the first time I had been blessed by Our Lady. I've been to Medjugorje four times. The first time it happened to be the thirty-fifth wedding anniversary of the couple I was traveling with. We were walking to mass, praying to the Blessed Mother, when I happened to look up over at Mount Krizevek. There, clearly, was an image of the Blessed Mother cradling her infant son, Jesus. The image was in cloud formation at least two hundred feet high, but it was as clear as if she were next to me. My friends followed my gaze, and they saw it too! We stood there praying and watching for more than five minutes, and as it faded, a cross took its place directly over the enormous cross at the peak of the mountain! That image of the Madonna is indelibly etched in my memory, one of the many special graces Our Lady has sent me.

My second trip was part of a pilgrimage for the Medjugorje Peace Conference, and it truly changed my life. People from all over the globe had come, dedicated to fostering Our Lady's message. The purpose of the trip was to determine how we could best serve her by spreading her word without distorting or changing the message. We were scheduled to meet with the visionaries themselves, and the Franciscans, to guide us in our mission.

Throughout this trip we were given so very many graces, and there is one that was particularly memorable. We had been graced with an invitation to be present in the choir loft during Our Lady's appearance. I truly cannot begin to describe what it was like to be kneeling seven feet away from where the Blessed Mother allegedly would be appearing! I was so overwhelmed I didn't know what to do! "Should I look up at the wall where she is to appear? Should I be looking at the visionaries? Someone please tell me what I should do!" were the kinds of thoughts racing through my mind.

And then this little voice within me spoke, saying, "Pray, you dummy! Start praying!" Of course! So I began to say the Hail Mary, suffused with the most awesome sense of peace I had ever experienced. Although I did not see the Blessed Mother, I did see the golden light descend into the room as she was appearing. Later we were told that

that light was from the two angels escorting her from heaven!

In helping to promote her message, I have written a pamphlet which I dedicated to the use of the world. I wrote it for young people to try to inspire faith in a generation that has a difficult world to contend with. I'm a grandmother now, and when I look at young parents trying to raise their children to be close to God, to be good, moral people, I know how hard that is, how much faith it takes. I want them to know that Our Lady can help. She is, after all, the Blessed Mother, and who better to turn to for guidance with our children?

That second trip to Medjugorje, for the pilgrimage, changed my life because I returned more dedicated than ever to be in service to Our Lady, and I have done that by sending seventy-five thousand of my pamphlets all over the world, from Iceland to Tahiti, New Guinea, Australia, everywhere. I even received a letter from a woman in Sri Lanka who wants to distribute them there.

The Blessed Mother is dedicated to getting her message out to all, and she can use even the most miserable of souls! I feel that helping to spread her word, helping to open hearts to her, has been my calling, but everyone can do something to help her share the glory of God. For the sake of our future generations, it is worth it.

FLORA BALDWIN
Garden Grove, California

THE BLESSED Virgin Mary, the Queen of Peace, it is told of her that she made her divine form appear to some in Pasadena, California, on the evening of June 24, 1989, who were gathered in celebration of the eighth anniversary of the apparitions in Medjugorje.

We were to partake in prayer and participate in a home mass. The service was conducted with piety, dignity, and energy, when from the balcony came a woman's cry, as from someone taken suddenly ill. The cry came again. I feared someone had been injured and had an impulse to move through the dense congregation crowded into the small apartment to the balcony to administer first aid of whatever form might have presented itself to my competence. But the press upon the space was great, and the mass was not yet brought to its holy completion.

I spied the balcony, and saw the people looking outward, and learned from one among us that some were seeing the Blessed Virgin in yonder trees! I did, by dint of effort, gain the balcony and followed the gaze of those looking out at a ten-degree right angle. I peered with my myopic eyes and saw a patch of light in an oval shape in a cluster of tree branches. It was an elongated patch of light as might be cast by the new, high-intensity gas lamps now coming into wide use for security.

A lady of the group began to direct my visual attention, describing to me in every intonation of certainty that the Blessed Virgin Mary was standing upon a globe, holding a baby in her arms. Another member of the congregation, a Filipino woman, came forth and proceeded to be my guide in further discerning the divine. Her description was similar to the other lady's in that the Madonna had the same veil and the babe, but hers was standing not upon a globe, but on a pedestal of light. These two women were honestly conveying what they truly saw and were generous in sharing with me what I might otherwise have failed to obtain in joy and grace.

My wife, Augustine, joined me on the balcony, and looked outward at an angle, too. She soon wore the expression of someone in a state of excitement and deep faith, but she said nothing. I expressed a desire to run downstairs and have a look at the image from a nearer vantage point, but she discouraged me with a warning from the Lord. "Thou shalt not tempt the Lord, your God," she said. Thus, to my consternation, I was compelled to avert myself from testing the miracle alleged to be in progress before us.

Voices on the darkened balcony discoursed on the apparition and those who could not see her stepped aside to make room for others. My wife and I remained with those enraptured by the visitation, and after some time had passed, I noticed with astonishment that a number of people inside the apartment were eating, drinking, and making merry. As I looked upon this scene of mixed reverence and gluttony, I could not help wondering how it would fall upon the heart of Christ that some among this assembly were ignoring His Blessed Mother. I took courage and began to lead a singing of "How Great Thou Art."

I kept my eyes straining on the patch of light during the singing of all four stanzas of the song, and I believe in all sincerity that I could make out her veil. It was dim, however, and out of respect to the divine and diverse agencies of heaven, I took care to admit that I am equally susceptible to the power of suggestion as any child of God, and so I did not congratulate myself on becoming a full visionary yet.

Some people said they saw two angels accompanying the Madonna. My wife later said that she had clearly seen two figures, smaller than the Blessed Virgin, who remained at her feet. I, myself, watched in amazement as the figure turned herself to the right. The sight of Mary, worldly spouse of Joseph and Mother of a famous Son, on one hand a mere fifty yards away and a few scant feet higher, commingled with people eating and drinking, made me feel that this is surely an age of folly and a dissolute generation.

Now this report may seem tinged with skepticism, but let me state clearly that I am far from that. I remain ever mindful of the foolish gentleman at

Fatima who derided the "superstitions" that held Portugal incarcerated in poverty. But he, upon witnessing the miracle of the sun as it hurled itself downward toward the seventy thousand people gathered on October 13, 1917, was one of the first to collapse on the ground in a penitent, public confession of his mistake. The millions who have read of this are well advised to avoid the errors of vain conceit, of pridefulness and disrespect to the Mother of God.

Those who know that they saw the Blessed Virgin are due the highest regard for holding Mary so forward on their minds. They are ready at every moment to behold a miracle, even in the midst of a technological, prosperous age. Surely, they, in turn, will never be forgotten by her.

One further note regarding that night. One among the celebrants was a woman who was alleged to be a visionary and the recipient of inner locutions. I was not aware of her presence until the appearance of Our Blessed Virgin. She apparently had been hemmed in on every side by the throng of people that can only be described as a veritable forest of bodies. Then, when the first cry rang out, heralding Mary's arrival, a force pushed Louise through the multitude. The power of that force reminded me of how the children of Medjugorje were enabled to scale the height of the hill of apparitions ahead of the villagers, who saw them raised up as if walking on air in order to meet the Blessed Virgin. And if we imagine the mount at the Sinai Monastery of St. Catherine, we can surmise that it was this same force of divine intercession that carried Moses up that sheer, inhospitable crag. "Angels will bear thee up, lest thou dash thy foot upon a stone," say the scriptures.

By such exalted stature do the creatures of heaven display their contempt for natural law. They are accountable only to a higher system that remains largely hidden from worldly eyes. Yet surely this is the very same order that the Blessed Virgin Mary hails from, and I support that universe with my continued faith and open heart.

ROBERT SUPIN
San Fernando, California

ON THE EVENING of June 24, 1989, my wife and I and four friends went to the Pasadena apartment of Rafael Blom to celebrate the eighth anniversary of the apparitions in Medjugorje, and to enjoy a potluck dinner afterward.

We arrived around seven o'clock. It didn't take long for the small apartment to become very crowded. I would say that there were about fifty people inside, and another thirty on the balcony where my wife and I had found two chairs available at a table.

The mass, which lasted for almost two hours—we prayed a full fifteen decades of the rosary—was conducted by Father Stacey. When it was almost over, the people on the right side of the balcony began to get restless. Someone leaned over and told me that the Blessed Mother was outside in the trees. I got up to move over to that side of the balcony, slowly making my way through the crowd.

It was then that I saw a beautiful white figure standing like a statue, only brilliant with brightness. The shape of the figure was similar to Our Lady as she appeared in Lourdes. She was not life-size, but smaller, and suspended in the branches of the trees across from the apartment building. I couldn't believe it, but there she was, before our eyes!

By this time everyone on the balcony had moved to the right side to get a better view, and others who had been inside were trying to get outside. My wife and I felt blessed that we had been able to see her, and so we began to edge our way back inside to avoid any problems with the crowd. Just before we were inside, I turned for one long, last look at the luminous figure in white. I saw her move, and in that instant, I knew without a doubt in my mind or my heart that Our Mother was here among us.

I then called out, my voice loud and clear, "She's moving!" because I understood that the Blessed Virgin Mary, by her movement, was telling us all that, "I am here, I am not an illusion."

Miraculously, there was never any panic, although one woman sobbed uncontrollably. But the rest of the group stayed quite calm throughout the visitation. It was late in the evening when the figure faded, leaving us all with a life-long belief that we each had experienced a great blessing.

ERNESTO LAGUETTE
Fullerton, California

I WAS REALLY devoted to the Virgin Mary at a very young age. For instance, instead of going out at recess to play, I would remain in the church at my Catholic school, lighting candles and praying. I felt so intensely close to her that when I was in the second grade, an incident occurred that I couldn't decide was real or a dream.

My family lived adjacent to a school yard with a large baseball field. Behind the field were woods and a large wire fence to delineate the school property. I found myself standing in the middle of the field, just off the pitcher's mound, when something started to approach me. It was a horribly frightening figure that I thought, at the time, was Satan, but in retrospect looked more like the Jolly Green Giant. I have since learned that this being is known all over Europe as the Green Man, and throughout history there have been reports and sightings of this Father Earth figure.

He ran up to me aggressively, and when he reached out to touch me, I was paralyzed with terror. I wanted to move, I wanted to run away from him, but I couldn't. I felt like there was no way out, nowhere for me to turn. That's when I looked up into the sky and there was the Virgin Mary descending in this very luminescent gold and white light. I awoke, and there she was in my room, exactly as I had seen her in my dream—if that's what it was. She was hovering above my bed surrounded by that radiant brightness. I was crying, but not from fear any longer. It was just so amazing to see her there before me.

The next day at school I spoke to one of my teachers, Sister Maria, and told her what had happened. She didn't know if my experience was real or a dream either, but she reassured me by saying that there was nothing for me to be afraid of. She was very supportive and loving, and the incident further deepened my love for the Virgin Mary.

The year before this occurred, I won a book-reading contest the nuns held. I read the most books within a specific period of time, and my best friend came in third. Technically, I got to choose the prize first, but my friend had a very persuasive personality. She promised me that if I'd let her have the beautiful Carmelite statue of the Virgin Mary that I wanted, she'd let me come to her swimming pool every day. She got the statue of the Virgin Mary, I ended up with a St. Anne statue that I didn't really care for, and I never once got to my friend's pool!

We remained close, though, and twenty years later, I asked her if she remembered the contest and the statue. She didn't, but around the time I was getting married, she hunted through her attic to find it and she sent it to me as a gift.

In high school, I left the church, shunned Catholicism and everything associated with it, including the Virgin Mary, and instead I started studying Eastern religions. I remained this way until recently.

In December 1994, a series of personal events befell me, leaving me traumatized and feeling very isolated. I was desperate for some guidance, and a friend recommended a healer. I had no idea what to expect, but I was desperate, so I called and she agreed to come to my home and try to help me.

When she arrived, the first thing I noticed was that she was wearing painted, wooden earrings with what looked like the Virgin Mary on them. And one of the first things she asked me was, "How do you feel about the Virgin Mary?" Then she said, "I have to be honest with you. I went into meditation this morning to see how I could help you and what came to me is that I need to tell you that the Virgin Mary is available to you for protection. She wants you to know that she is here for you now."

I was startled because it had been such a long time since I had abandoned the Blessed Mother. I told the healer then about my childhood experience and how I had later turned away from Mary. The woman took from her purse a holy card with an image of the Virgin Mary on it, which she had come across in a bookstore years earlier and had been saving all this time. In it, the Virgin had blond hair and blue eyes, which is an unusual depiction of the Madonna, but I have blond hair and blue eyes! The healer had been told that morning, in her meditation, to give me the holy card.

In the weeks to come, I began to realize that the Virgin Mary has been with me all this time that I thought I had left her. The statue coming back to me after so much time was one example. I had pictures of icons on my desk and around my house that I had collected when I was in Russia. I had never consciously acknowledged these signs that I still felt close to Mary, but I did now, thankful that she protected me when I believed I was alone, and thankful, too, that I could once again welcome her back into my life.

CYNTHIA LAZAROFF
Pacific Palisades, California

WHAT OCCURRED to me and my wife has changed our lives. We have been blessed with a kind of grace, and I would like to share with you exactly what happened.

It was March 5, around seven thirty at night. I was watching a basketball game on television when I sensed the presence of somebody with me, which unnerved me since my wife and children were out. The feeling was so strong that I got up to look around and that's when the mirror in my bedroom caught my attention, for in it was an image of the Blessed Mother!

I quickly determined that the image was actually coming from the blinds behind me, so ethereal, like a shadow, yet unmistakably the Blessed Mother. She was about five feet tall and I could distinguish her facial features, even her hands and fingers, that's how clear the image was. I couldn't believe what I was seeing, how much my heart was racing with such joy.

I approached her slowly and spent two hours talking and praying with her. It was the most extraordinary experience of my life! When my wife came home at nine thirty I called out for her to come quickly to our room. I said nothing. I didn't have to. The moment she entered, she cried out, "It is her! It is really her!" Together with our children, we stayed and prayed to the Blessed Mother until one o'clock in the morning, thanking her for giving us the gift of her visit.

The next day we shared our experience with a few close friends who wanted to come over and see where the Holy Virgin had been. We wanted to be generous with what had been given us, so we welcomed everyone. To our amazement, and everlasting gratitude, the Blessed Mother returned the next evening at the same time, and now others could see her and feel her loving presence.

And for eighty-seven miraculous days, the Blessed Mother continued to visit our home!

Word spread, of course, and my wife and I tried to keep a tally of how many people came to see her. We know it was around eight thousand six hundred, and sometimes it was up to five hundred a day! A few came more than once, hoping to be healed. The Blessed Mother did not appear only to visionaries, either. We would clearly see her move and face sideways; we saw a profile of Jesus looking over at his Mother; we were also given an image of her as the Queen of Peace.

When the media heard about it, they, of course, wanted to disprove everything, claiming that the image was projected from somewhere, or a man-made light was reflecting off a statue. We let them come, too, but they found nothing to substantiate their claims. And other incidents occurred that proved how very special these eighty-seven days were for everyone.

At one point during her stay, three white doves appeared over our house. Then, for three nights, a big star could be seen above our home. People who had been out of work for a long time, trying to find a job, found jobs. And the healing from within has been the most special gift she left for us.

My wife and children and I tend to devote more time to our spiritual lives now. Some things we continue to sense from within, and we know that she is always with us, protecting us, blessing us. In return, I try to speak at churches and religious groups as much as I can, to tell people about our eighty-seven days of grace so that others will know that the Blessed Mother can come for anyone.

FREDDIE GALAZ
Las Cruces, New Mexico

I COME FROM four generations of Scottish seers, although I was born in Mexico where three generations of my family have lived. We have always had a relationship to spirit, one of active dialogue, conversations. Personally, I've had thirty years of experiences and encounters, primarily with angels and devas. I have never once begun a session or a meditation without first petitioning the office of the Spiritual Mother for permission, because I believe with all my heart that she is the woman I am here on earth to work for.

I am a Guadalupano, and last year, the Virgin blessed me with a visit. I had known of her presence with me on an intuitive level for many, many years, but to finally see her was, I believe, a gift from her for never wavering in my faith.

My first psychic experience occurred when I was eight years old. It had to do with a feminine spirit known in Mexico as La Llorona, the Crying Woman.

There was a myth about her that she had once drowned her two children in a river, and so Mexican mothers would always tell their children that "La Llorona will get you if you're not good." When I saw her, all the kids I was with ran from the room in terror, but I stayed and watched her float by. She was wearing a skirt, with a shawl wrapped around her, and she drifted just a few feet above the ground, but she had no legs. She just wafted on the air. After this, I was convinced that La Llorona was wondrous and certainly nothing to fear.

Eventually, as I grew up and studied and became more in touch with my spirituality and my legacy as a seer, I came to see La Llorona as the Mother of two civilizations suffering through invasion and change. The Indian religion was being destroyed and the Catholic religion, in its early stages, was not strongly Marian. It took a while for devotion to the Virgin to spread, and so I believe that La Llorona weeps for a healing of the two civilizations, floating from culture to culture on a pilgrimage of healing.

There is actually some historic precedent behind this myth: When Cortez came to Mexico, he found a young Aztec princess whose mother had sold her as a slave to a Mayan king. She spoke Mayan and Aztec, and there was also a Spaniard who spoke Mayan and Spanish, and together, these two served as translators for Cortez during his invasion of Mexico. Today, Mexicans often speak of this princess as La Chingada, which is a slang expression for "screwed up"— but I see her differently. Here was a young woman who had been sold out, not only by her own people, but by her own family, and when the fair-haired men came speaking of their One God, their Prince of Peace, she went with them as an act of liberation. Mexicans hold La Chingada in low regard, as they fear La Llorona, but I see two women who are very misunderstood.

Interestingly, the Virgin of Guadalupe appeared to an Indian, and spoke to him in his own language. The collective consciousness of the Native Indians was being subjugated by an Indo-Aryan society, and here is this woman bringing healing to her two children of two violently divided cultures. That is why I see La Llorona and Mary as connected, with La Llorona almost heralding what Mary would bring years later.

I have been a Guadalupano for many years, and I've made a pilgrimage of several hundred miles from Pueblow to Mexico City. This is a group pilgrimage on an intense spiritual quest. The vision is set, the journey is planned, and between the starting place and the end, atop a hillside sanctuary, is the quest. This has become a rite of passage as a way to present yourself to the Virgin. Many of the natives and Catholics, too, believe that the suffering along the arduous journey is an individual, as well as collective, transmutation of sin for the community. After the Industrial Revolution, there has been such hyper-individualization that people have been left feeling isolated and alone. Yet on this quest, I was often in tears brought on by the sense of community. At the time, I was a teenager and a warrior who could protect the elders, and I could also help carry the young ones because I had the strength to do so. I was accepted in all these roles by the community despite being so different from them. I was about two and a half feet taller than everyone else, not to mention blond and fair skinned. And I wasn't Catholic!

Pilgrimages are still being done, and here in New Mexico, the women walk the many miles from Ojo Caliente to the Santuario de Chimayo, carrying the banner of the Virgin. Several of my American, non-Catholic friends have been accepted by them on these walks, too.

We live in a culture of instant gratification, where there is little patience for that walk, the journey, the quest to unfold. We like revelation without undergoing the real spiritual growth that takes place through every path we take in life. I believe, therefore, that my own personal encounter with the Virgin was a kind of reward for never wavering in my faith. It was confirmation of a Celtic lesson, which is that one has to be constantly aware that you see in spirit with your heart, not with your eyes. So even though for years I did not see the Divine Mother, she has been with me all along.

I have been out lecturing and giving workshops for many years now, to help people continue to grow after they receive a divine gift. When someone is blessed with a vision or a spiritual experience, it should become a gateway to further spiritual evolvement, so I try to give people a map, you might say, for doing that in their lives.

I remember something that I learned about thirty years ago that I feel is very germane to understanding the Virgin. I had been curious at the time about my guardian angel, and I wanted to know his or her name. I went into meditation, and was told that by naming something or overpersonalizing this divine being, its function would become limited. Mary has been given many names over the years so that we can anchor our gratitude and devotion to her. But I think we should leave ourselves open to the mystery of her spirit by any name, and just see where that leads us.

KIP DAVIDSON
Ojo Caliente, New Mexico

MY STORY begins when I was two and a half years old. I was staying at my cousin's house in what, to me, was a really dire situation. There were seven boys, all older than me, and I remember this one afternoon when there was a lot of rough-housing going on around me. I crouched under a chair, wondering if I could make it across the room without getting knocked over. I was feeling so lonely and desolate, like I was in the worst danger and nobody cared. As I was crunched there, I found myself looking up at a painting of a beautiful woman who had tears streaming down her face. Her hands were clasped together and whatever she was looking at made her really sad, but even in her grief there was something so beautiful about her that I could not stop staring. Although I was barely a toddler, it was a really spiritual experience. A deep, sweet peace came out from that image and enfolded me, and I knew then that I would be safe. I believed that this lady, whoever she was, was my friend and that she would protect me. Throughout the rest of that visit, I would go and sit under that chair and look at her picture whenever I needed to, and she made me feel so safe.

When I was a little older, about five or six, I used to see Mary walking around my family's yard, and I felt that she was my friend. Then, as I started to grow up, going to school and doing things with other children my age, Mary and her friendship faded away, although I still had a sense that she was with me at night.

Like many teenagers, I went through a period of rebellion—from the time I was fourteen until I was about twenty-two. I really turned away from everything: I didn't believe in God, I was very angry, and I didn't think about Mary anymore. I had rejected everything, but I noticed that there seemed to be a force of protection operating in my life. I seemed to be safe from harm, especially the kind I was apt to bring upon myself. Today I call it a force of grace—

and I know that Mary did not abandon me, even when I had turned away from her.

Years later I found myself called to develop my psychic abilities, and I trained for five years to direct this faculty to help others. I continue to do this, with clients and through my book, *The Kitchen Mystic*.

It wasn't until 1982, though, that Mary consciously came back into my life. I was having a dream, a really wonderful dream, where I was in a room and this beautiful woman walked in and gazed upon me with tremendous love. She didn't look like the classic depictions of Mary, although she was wearing long blue robes. The woman had modern-style hair and manicured fingernails and wore pretty rings on her hands. I watched, amazed, as she glided up to me. She knelt down before me, clasping my feet and looking up into my eyes. Then this river of energy shot up my legs from her hands and ran up my whole spine. It was a beautiful wellspring of peace that rushed into my body from her touch and from her eyes.

I changed after that dream. I began to see this deep, beautiful Mary-blue light in the periphery of my vision. And I began to hear a soft, gentle, nurturing voice, whispering guidance intuitively to help me and guide me.

I trusted the Lady implicitly. I could feel that she was perfect, the absence of ego in her energy making her a perfected being. She guided me this way for four years, never leading me wrong about anything, and always totally accurate, be it about my own life or more global situations. Finally, at a Spiritual Frontiers Fellowship Conference I was attending, she revealed herself to me.

A woman was coming on to the stage to speak to the audience and she was kind of flabbergasted as she began because, she said, Mary and Jesus had both just appeared to her while she was waiting backstage, and that had never happened to her before. While this woman was giving the audience their message, I heard the soothing voice of my guide, the Lady.

"That's me. I'm Mother Mary."

I was incredulous, of course, although I now know I shouldn't have been. "You're Mother Mary?" I asked.

"Yes, that's me."

"You're kidding! Are you sure?"

"Yes, I'm Mary."

"You mean, like the Mother of Christ? You mean, the Blessed Virgin Mary?"

"Yes, that's me."

Finally, I accepted that this had to be her, because I was being so stubborn and so difficult and so skeptical and her patience never wavered. Only someone as perfect and generous as Mary could be so patient!

When I began to hear about Medjugorje and Mary's appearances there, I wanted that, too. I wanted to see *her*, not just the blue light. I remember asking, "What about me? Why don't you appear to me?" Then one night when I fell asleep on my couch, I awoke in the middle of the night to the sound of wind gusting through my living room. Even though the windows were closed, I could actually feel the wind blowing; it was kind of a wet, damp wind, and I could smell mountain air and rocks and flowers. I pried my eyes open and saw, across the room, a figure in white, beaming in like on *Star Trek*, with white sparkles filling in her space. I just totally freaked out, yelling, "Wait! Wait! I'm not ready! I'm not ready." But I had asked to see her and so she had come.

After this incident, though, I didn't feel ready to see her again for a long time.

She has appeared twice, in the Northern Lights. Once, I was walking at night with two friends, having the kind of inner dialogue with the Lady that I had been having for years, only this time I found myself saying, "You know, I really would like to see you sometime." A voice very distinctly answered: "Well, turn around and look at the Northern Lights."

The three of us turned around. I saw only the lights, but they fell to their knees as they saw Mary! I told myself that this was preparation, that she knew I still wasn't ready. Then I saw a shooting star flash through the lights, but my two friends gasped with astonishment, telling me that they had seen her very clearly lift her hand to her heart and fling that star out into the night! I saw the star. I saw the lights. But I still didn't see Mary.

Finally, a year later, I was out in the country with a friend. We saw the Northern Lights and stopped to get out of the car. I felt surrounded by Mary's energy. I knew she was present, and this time, I thought, "Okay, I'm ready—I can see you now." Then this light gathered in the sky and grew and grew until a huge image formed—a very clear image of a person in a long gown whose arms were extended outward to the heavens. My friend saw it too! The whole sky was ablaze with her light from horizon to horizon, and it flabbergasted me to think about how powerful she really is. Then, as quickly as she had appeared, the image faded and was gone.

Mary also intervenes specifically in my electronic life, playing with things like my computer, or my phone.

One morning I was driving my daughter to daycare and I was very sleepy. I made a wrong turn and was stopped by the police. I knew I was in big trouble because I already had two outstanding traffic tickets. I couldn't handle the idea of dragging the baby downtown to pay my fines, not on this particular morning.

That's when I found myself saying out loud, "I can't handle this! I really can't handle this right now!" The police officer went back to his patrol car to call in for a computer search on my license, but he couldn't find a record of me anywhere. All he did was issue a summons and let me go. But as I drove off, there was Mother Mary saying, "Don't worry, it's okay, but go downtown and pay your tickets later today." Which I did, all three of them.

Another time I was talking to my sister on the telephone when I began to say something that would have betrayed a confidence given me by our brother. My sister later told me that she heard me say, "Well, it's like this . . ." then five minutes of static, and finally, "So that's all it was." Throughout the static she kept calling my name, but I never heard her. I did hear Mother Mary, though, saying, "You know, you really can't do that." She was protecting me from my own mistakes. She would not let me hurt anyone, so she just bleeped the phone line.

There was another interesting intervention I would like to share. I went to Victoria's Secret, of all places, to buy some lingerie. I fell in love with a camisole that was too expensive, but I just couldn't seem to let it go. I knew that I didn't want to spend more than twenty-five dollars, and the camisole was more than twice that. I finally made up my mind to go for it, but when the sales person entered the tag into the computer, the price came out as twenty-five dollars! Now, there was no way to mistake what was printed on the tag. It said the price of the camisole was fifty-six dollars, but the manager of the store came over and said, "Well, if the computer thinks it's only twenty-five dollars, then I'm not going to bother you about it!" I knew exactly who had been playing with that computer.

So these are some of the little gifts and surprises that Mother Mary brings to me. I am constantly amazed at how present she is in my life. She is like a good mother who is paying very close attention to her child. She is so sensitive and she wants everyone to know that anyone who needs a spiritual Mom can have her!

MARY HAYES-GRIECO
Minneapolis, Minnesota

JUST A FEW years ago, when I was twenty-one, I was going through a period of very serious confusion. I was in college, but not fully pleased with my field of study, which was English literature. I felt as if this wasn't my true calling, but I didn't know exactly what that might be. I was at a crossroads without having any idea which direction to take. I desperately needed some clarity in my life.

I received the guidance and the subsequent insight on a bitterly frigid winter evening. There was an unusually solemn stillness in the air which struck me as particularly suitable to the occasion. Two friends and I were visiting another friend who had recently lost his father in a bizarre auto accident. He was run down by a truck, and his death—so unexpected, so sudden—filled me with a strong awareness of the impermanence of life. Here it was this most special gift of all, and I didn't know what to do with mine!

The most amazing thing happened as we stepped into the house. We were on our way in when my friend turned to me and said, "Jesus and Mary are with you tonight." She spoke in this peculiar prophetic tone I had never heard from her before, as if what she said were from an angelic messenger. I just froze there on the landing, waiting to see if there was more to this divine message, but she said nothing else and we just walked into the house.

After dinner, we remained at the dining room table and we lit a candle, a black candle, merely to shed light in the now dimmed room. For some time now, I had been praying for clarity and as I sat at my friend's dinner table, with that black candle flickering in the low winter light, I began to pray, with my eyes closed, for healing—for my friend, the one whose father had died. When I opened my eyes, I was gazing into the candle, the flames dancing and flickering, creating shadows on the walls.

I watched the dancing shadows and saw that they had turned to stone, and standing there among the shadows was a beautiful woman. I was aware, too, that I had left my body. I was no longer in the room with my friends, but in a cave with a huge fire in the center. Emerging from the darkness was the Blessed Mother. I knew it was her immediately, because her radiance outshone even the brightest flames of the fire.

I stared, unblinking, and that's when I realized that the Virgin Mary was appearing to me as the Black Madonna. Her robes were black, as deep as the night sky, but accented by the golden blaze of a million stars. She looked upon me with such under-standing and love that I felt redeemed. I could tell that she knew I was lost and wanted me to know that she was with me, to guide and help.

Wordlessly, she beckoned me to her and she then placed her hand upon my forehead. I felt as if she were knowingly putting my fears to rest, clearing my mind of its confusions and doubts. Intu-itively, I determined that she wanted me to lie down, which I did, and then she sprinkled something over my body. Afterward, a great peace descended upon me. There was no question in my mind that every-thing in my life would now be fine.

As I came back from my vision, I saw that the flame of the black candle had burned down about half-way, and oddly, there was a large piece of wax clinging to the right side of the candle. I looked closer and noticed that the wax looked like a minia-ture statue of what I had just seen—the Black Madonna. She wore the same billowing black robes, and was gazing into the fire just as she had in my vision. As comforting and confirming of the apparition as this was for me, it was not the only one. As we left for the evening, the same friend who had earlier heralded this mystical experience, asked me, "Did anyone else see Mary in the candle?"

Our host let me take the candle home, and that night marked the beginning of my new life. I dropped out of college for a year, the first step of the spiritual journey that will last the rest of my life.

I had always wanted to be an artist, but I never had the confidence to pursue it, unsure that I would be successful. After this year of personal inquiry and discovery, a year that I never, ever would have had the courage to embark on had it not been for my encounter with the Blessed Mother, I enrolled in art school and today I am pleased to say that I now design jewelry for a living. I love what I'm doing, and people think I'm really good at it too! She gave me guidance, insight, and most of all, the courage to believe in myself—exactly when I needed those strengths most.

That black candle with the wax that looked like a miniature statue of the Black Madonna? I still have it, on my altar as a constant reminder of Mary's guiding presence.

KRISTIN PAMPERIN
Weehawken, New Jersey

HEALINGS

Many seke ben here cured by our Lady's myghte;
Dede agayne revyved of this no dought;
Lame made whole and blynded restored to syghte
Lo here the chyef solace agaynste all tribulacyon;
To all that be seke bodely or goostly;
Callin' to Our Lady devoutly.

RICHARD PYNSON

TWENTY YEARS ago I was a young nun, very happy with my calling to be of service to others in life. It was what I had always wanted and I felt particularly lucky that I had been accepted into the order. Too soon, however, the life I had envisioned for myself developed first one crack, then another, until it lay in pieces around me.

I was diagnosed as having multiple sclerosis. In due time, it became bad enough to keep me from living and contributing fully to the religious life. I was granted a dispensation from my vows and returned to my parents' home in Iowa. I realized that I couldn't stay there since they had five younger children to take care of, but when I went out looking for a job, I couldn't get one. I couldn't get health or medical insurance either because my illness was considered a preexisting condition.

I was terribly unhappy. I felt such a keen sense of disappointment and loss. All I had ever wanted was to be of service as a nun, and now that had been taken from me.

I went to my family doctor, who was also a good friend, and he spoke to me as such: "I want you to leave Iowa and go some place where no one knows you and start your life all over again. You may have another five or so good years left and you should really live them and enjoy them."

I did just that, moving to Pennsylvania where I received a job offer as a teacher from the Butler County Special Education Department. It was a standard part of the hiring process at the time for prospective teachers to have a physical. My doctor back home had advised me not to tell them I had MS, but to say that I had been afflicted with polio as a child. This would explain any problems with my reflexes and any abnormalities on the neurological part of the exam. This may seem slightly unethical, but really, it wasn't. First of all, the advice had not been given to me by my physician, so to speak, but by a man who cared about my welfare in a far more subjective sense. Secondly, although my conscience did have more than a slight twinge at not being totally forthright with my new employers, I knew I had so little productive time left, and nothing mattered as much to me as being a productive, contributing member of society. So I did what my doctor-friend had suggested, and I was hired.

I was teaching special education in a small school in Mars, Pennsylvania, when I met my husband-to-be. For a few years we were just very good friends, not romantically involved, and I never told him that I had MS. When he asked me why I wore those funny-looking orthopedic shoes and why I sometimes tripped, I again used the excuse that a bout with childhood polio had left a few residual effects. When he did ask me to marry him, though, I still didn't tell him! In my own mind, I rationalized that maybe I would be like some people who only have one attack of the disease, so why bring up something that might never really become an issue? I could get lucky, too, couldn't I?

And I was, for the first two years of our marriage. We were both in our midthirties by this time, more than ready to start a family. We wanted children desperately, and when I couldn't get pregnant, I went to see a doctor about it. After he examined me, he said, "There is something the matter with you and I think you know what it is. I really would not recommend that you have children. I would, however, recommend that you find a good neurologist and start making provisions for what may happen in the future." I promptly changed doctors!

Within three months I was pregnant with Kristin. I was told not to have any more children, of course, so within three years we had two more little girls, Ellen and Heidi. I had quit teaching to become a full-time mother, and still I did not tell my husband or children about my condition. After Heidi's birth, however, I could no longer say that my lack of coordination was attributable to polio, because now other symptoms of MS started to manifest themselves. I was unable to raise my hands above my head. I tripped often. I fell. I could not walk more than one hundred to two hundred feet without help. Needless to say, my husband was horribly worried about me, but neither of us would talk about it. Finally, one day I had a severe attack and he took me to the hospital, where the doctors told me that I was gravely ill. Even then I refused to accept what they were telling me. I just turned my head to the wall and cried. I cried out for what my husband would do when I finally told him the truth; I cried for my three children because I couldn't be the mother I'd wanted to be for them; and I cried for myself, for the imperfect future that awaited me.

The doctors discharged me, and once home, my husband and I had our first really honest talk. I told him about my condition. I tried to explain why I had kept the truth from him. When I finished, my husband asked for a divorce. I will never forget that day as long as I live. He left the house and I sat there and cried my heart out for everything that had gone so wrong.

Amazingly, my husband came home within three or four hours. He was so subdued as he spoke.

"I know that I may not be able to handle this, but I'm going to try," he said to me. "Just don't ask me to make any promises right now—we'll have to see how it goes." From that moment on, he became the most supportive, the most wonderful, loving, generous-spirited human being I have ever known!

My disabilities worsened. It would take me two and a half to three hours just to make hamburgers and set them on the table—the simplest tasks taking all my concentration and effort. I also developed what is known as a valgus deformity, in which my right leg turned inward and the knee cap became completely dislocated off the surface of the knee, causing intense pain with every movement. My movement was restricted even further and so I went to an orthopedic surgeon who performed a retinacula release to free the knee cap, and allow it to follow the rest of the leg over to the side. With the aid of crutches, I managed, in my lurching gait, to take care of my home and children.

By 1982, I could no longer do for myself, and so a young lady who lived down the street began to come and help during the week. As good as she was, her presence only added to the guilt consuming me for knowing that my husband and children were not getting from me what they deserved, what they were entitled to. I was so upset and afraid, I began to bargain with God! "Dear God, please don't let this get any worse. Please! I'll do anything you want—just leave my hands and arms alone." When the MS entered my arms, and my fingers went numb, I pleaded some more. "Please God, just leave me alone from the neck up!"

I was angry and frustrated all the time. Within two short years, I had gone from one attack to another, crutches to wheelchair, a victim of a disease that was destroying me and those I loved. I just couldn't understand why this had happened to me, nor could I accept the limitations it imposed on me. I remember one Christmas in particular when the children were decorating the tree: I didn't think they were putting on the tinsel right and I sat there in my wheelchair getting angrier and angrier at what I thought was a mess—when, in truth, everything looked great. I decided to get up on my crutches to show them how to make the tree beautiful.

I wore steel braces up to my hips by now, so it was no small feat to get the crutches and then balance myself to stand up, but I did it. I then tried to reach forward to place some tinsel on the branch, but I lost my balance and teetered head first into the tree! Of course the children began to laugh, but all I could do, out of frustration, was cry. I remember banging my head and crying, "This is rotten, God, this is such a rotten disease!"

Depression and anger and impatience took over—with myself most of all. This wasn't a life, this was barely an existence, I thought. And even though I tried to convince myself that I had so much for which to be grateful—three wonderful children and a husband whose strength and support sustained me every day—I could only think of everything I didn't have and my turmoil was eating away at me.

Then one day a friend of mine called to say that there was going to be a healing mass at St. Ferdinand's and she invited me along. I told her that I would be too embarrassed to stand up in front of all those people. Although my friend kept persisting, it was my husband who convinced me to go. "Is it going to hurt you?" he said. "God knows all the doctors in the world haven't been able to help you one bit!" So I decided to attend.

When we arrived at the church, it was packed. I was in my braces, on my crutches, swinging myself up the aisle behind an usher who led me to a pew. The mass began almost immediately after the rosary and the concelebrants, myself included, were going up the aisle. All of a sudden I felt myself touched on the shoulders. I turned around and looked up to see a big, red-faced priest praying over me. All the other concelebrants just stood there and watched. I was absolutely mortified with embarrassment that I had been singled out in front of all these people.

Then, almost immediately it seemed, a sense of peace came over me unlike anything I had felt in years. I found myself praying to be able to accept God's will and be happy with whatever he had in store for me. After that mass, my life began to change. I stopped bargaining with God and instead learned to accept whatever he wanted for me. My illness was no longer going to be an excuse for me to avoid the service in life I so enjoyed. Once I surrendered my will to His, and once I understood and accepted that he had a purpose for me, my true healing began.

My husband noticed my change—how could he help but notice it when our home life entered a whole new phase of serenity and calm. I also decided that I had had enough of staying home. I had been a good teacher once and I could be a good teacher again, but that turned out to be easier said than done! I would go out for the interview, arranged by phone after someone read my resume, and then once they would see me, it was "thanks, but no thanks." I finally called my pastor and said, "Father, I need a job. I'm a good teacher and I know I could work well for you."

"It's funny you should call me today," he answered. "Two of my teachers just gave notice that they're not returning next year. Why don't you come by this afternoon?"

I had gotten hand controls for the car so I was able to drive myself over to the rectory, and that very afternoon I signed a contract to teach at St. Gregory's School!

For several years things were really great. I loved teaching, I loved being able to do something that I did well and that served a purpose for others. Nothing delighted me as much as being needed! But then, in 1985, the MS struck again, a very serious attack. It left me completely paralyzed from the waist down. I couldn't wiggle my toes; I couldn't move my feet; I had no sensation up my legs. The deformity in my right leg got worse, too, and the leg constantly buckled, unable to take any support whatsoever.

I spent four weeks as a patient at the Harmerville Rehabilitation Hospital, undergoing intensive therapy and gait training. After those four weeks, I returned every ninety days as an out-patient. I could no longer push a regular wheelchair, so I had to get a special lightweight, electric model and was trained to use that. A wheelchair elevator, grab rails, and everything else I needed to function was installed in the school, and we made plans to do the same at home. Now, a few years back, all this would have left me so despondent that I'm sure I would have just felt like flinging up my hands and giving up, but because of my renewed understanding and acceptance of the power and purpose of God's will, I was able to move on with my life despite the latest handicaps and readjustments.

One day I was reading *Readers Digest* when I saw this article about the Blessed Mother appearing to six youngsters in Medjugorje, Yugoslavia. I found it fascinating, but really didn't think much more about it until a book I had recently ordered arrived.

I had ordered a biography of Sister Lucy from Trinity Publications. So there it was, but there was also a notice from the publisher saying they owed me nine dollars. I knew they didn't owe me anything so I considered it a computer oversight and just ignored it. A week and a half later, another notice came in the mail asking if I wanted to donate the nine dollars they owed me. Well, being a school teacher with lots of medical costs and three children, etc., etc., I figured charity begins at home!

I was going through their catalogue, and that's when I saw it staring out at me: *Is the Blessed Mother Really Appearing in Medjugorje* by Father Rene Laurentin. The cost was $6.95 plus $2.00 in shipping and handling. I ordered it and figured that the publisher could keep the nickel! I was startled when the book arrived in about four or five days instead of the six to eight weeks each shipment usually took. I began to read immediately, and I couldn't put the book down.

I was deeply moved—so much so that I began to fast as she had asked in her messages to the children, and I ate only bread and water on Wednesdays and Fridays. The next time I went for a check-up my doctor was thrilled because I had lost fifteen pounds, which I definitely needed to lose! Even though I took in only eight hundred calories a day, my metabolism was down to zilch because I had no physical activity in my life.

Now, I usually went to bed around ten, my husband helping me up the steps by lifting one leg at a time until we reached the second floor. He would then go back downstairs to watch the news and I used that time alone for my prayers and spiritual reading. It was a treasured time alone for me, with the children in bed, and the house quiet. On June 18, 1986, at around eleven thirty at night, I had just finished my rosary when I heard a voice saying, "Why don't you ask?" "Ask what?" I wondered, and then, the words just spilled forth from me:

"Dear Mary, Queen of Peace, whom I believe is appearing to the six children at Medjugorje, would you please ask your Son to heal me anywhere I need to be healed. I know your Son said that if you have faith and you say to that mountain, 'Move!' that it will move. I believe. Please help me anywhere my faith is not strong."

When I finished, I felt a peculiar sensation of warmth throughout my body, as if an electric current was running from top to bottom. I must have fallen asleep because the next thing I knew it was six thirty in the morning and it was business as usual. My husband helped me dress, we put the wheelchair in the car, and off I went to school. A girl was there to help me and she got me situated in class. As far as I was concerned, everything was still "normal." As the morning went on, I began to notice an itching in my feet. I was so surprised and fascinated by the feeling that I waved Laverne off during the morning break, when she would normally have taken me to another building with a wheelchair accessible restroom.

I thought it was strange, of course, and as I bent down to scratch, I felt my toes in those big, clumsy, *thick*, orthopedic shoes go up and down, up and down! I was absolutely flabbergasted! I had seen several doctors and had more than one electromyography done—a medical procedure to scan for nerve activity in a limb. The results were always unanimous: I had absolutely no nerve activity anywhere in my legs. Consequently, there was no physical therapy that could help. Yet when I bent down to scratch, I could feel! I could actually feel! I also had feeling on the sides of my legs, which had been like blocks of wood before. I was beside myself with excitement!

I couldn't wait for class to be over—I sat there the whole time just wiggling my toes. When it finally ended, I drove home, so eager to see the expression on my husband's face when he saw what I could do. But the driveway was empty—no one was home. I had been complaining that strawberry season was almost over and we didn't have any berries, so I assumed that he and the kids had gone off to the berry farm for me. I would just have to wait.

My crutches had been left on a railroad tie so that I could reach them from the car. Normally, I would never attempt to climb the three steps up to the house unless someone was there to help me because my balance was so poor, but I had a real problem right now. The paralysis had left me with neurogenic bladder and bowel disorder secondary to the MS, meaning I had no control over when I was going or when I was stopping. And I had been so dumb-founded by my toes moving and the sensations I was feeling that I had sent Laverne off without taking my bathroom break. That meant I was wearing the same protection now, at one thirty in the afternoon, that I had put on at seven thirty in the morning. I had to get into the house and use the bathroom—*now!*

I got out of the car and picked up my crutches. "Well," I thought. "If you can wiggle your toes and feel the sides of your legs, maybe you can get up those steps!" I swung my left leg—that could bend—up, while my right leg, the one with the knee deformity, was locked in a stiff brace that went all the way up to my hip. So as my left leg went up, the right one just naturally followed, and sure enough I made it into the house.

It was very hot, so I decided to remove my braces and lie down on the daybed until my husband came home. I was so excited thinking how I was going to give him the show of his life. I knew he was going to be surprised, but I never could have figured on how surprised until I bent over to undo the steel keepers and the buckles that locked the braces in place. I didn't recognize my leg! I just stared and stared at my right leg as if it belonged to someone else, some stranger lying there. I remember screaming, "Oh my God! My God! My leg is straight!" It was perfectly straight—even my knee was in front where it belonged.

I truly was in a state of shock. I knew a miracle had taken place, but it hadn't quite sunk in yet. I do remember that I was wearing a rather long skirt and I picked up the hem and tucked it into my waistband so I could walk around on my crutches and watch the leg move! I just went from room to room in the house, crying and thanking the Blessed Mother until I reached the steps in the main hall that led to the second floor. As I stood there staring at those steps, I understood at last what had happened to me the night before. My sudden prayer; that electric feeling in my legs: I had been healed! And as understanding dawned, so did the realization that if I'm healed, I can *run* up those stairs!

And I did! I placed the crutches in the corner and I ran up those steps! As I got to the top I started jumping up and down, screaming with such joy that it's really impossible to describe in words. I then ran back downstairs, threw open the front door and went outside. I was hysterical, running so many times around the house that our dog started to chase me, and all I kept saying over and over was, "Thank you, God! Thank you, Blessed Mother!"

Finally, I calmed down long enough to go back into the house. Of course I couldn't contain myself. I had to tell somebody, and the first person I thought of was my pastor. The minute he answered the phone, I shouted: "I'm healed! I'm healed! I don't have MS anymore!"

"Who is this?" he asked.

"I don't have MS anymore! I've been healed!"

"Is this Rita?"

"Yes! Yes!"

"Rita, sit down and take two aspirin and call your doctor. Now will you do that, please?" Do you know what I did? I hung up on him, thinking he was no help whatsoever! The next person I thought to call was my neighbor, the one who had taken me to the healing mass, but by the time I reached her, I couldn't even speak I was crying so badly. Somehow she understood that it was me and before I knew it, she was at my house, staring frozen as I jumped up and down all over my living room! "Why are you just standing there!" I cried out. "Look at me! Just look at me!"

That snapped her out of shock, and she ran over to hug me and we both started screaming and crying and jumping all around. "We have to go find Ron and the girls!" she said. We found a pair of my daughter's sandals that fit, and off we went, but first we stopped at the rectory so that I could show my pastor in person what had happened. He was standing in his study when I ran in. I will never forget the look on his face as I knelt down without any help and asked him for his blessing. I felt as if I were seventeen. Even now I can't describe the energy flowing through me after years and years of the horrible weakness and fatigue the paralysis had created. It was like being reborn.

By the time we got to the strawberry farm, it had closed and everyone had gone home. I remember pulling into the driveway of our house and seeing my husband walk out the front door. His face was chalky white, and he seemed to be in a daze. I realized, of course, that he must have come home, seen the empty car with the wheelchair still in the back seat, my empty braces in the house, my crutches in the hallway—and thought something terrible had happened to me and that I had been taken to the hospital.

You can only imagine the scene of pandemonium when I got out of the car! My children were particularly unnerved by my running up and down the hill to the woods and dancing the Irish jig. They had never known me as anything but handicapped. They had never had a mother who could bowl or golf or even shop with them. Eventually, we all calmed down long enough for my husband to call the doctor. Ron explained that I wasn't using my wheelchair or my crutches anymore. He told him that I didn't need them—I was walking without them! "That's totally impossible!" the doctor stated. "That's not all of it," my husband went on. "She's *running*. She's running up and down the hill and all over the place!" "That can't be," the doctor argued. "There is no way she can do that." He wanted to see me right away, of course.

He was very polite when we got there, but after just a few moments of small talk, said, "Well, I'm busy and I have to go back to work now." Ron asked why he didn't want to examine me, and he said, "Oh, I went over what you said with some of the other doctors and this is Rita's sister, right? Her twin sister?" He thought we were playing a joke on him. It really took quite a bit of convincing—and demonstrating— until he accepted that it was really me. The children helped by saying, "This is really our mom! She doesn't have any sisters that look like her. They have black hair and live in Iowa and that's far from here!"

When he finally examined me, he couldn't believe, let alone understand, what he found: everything he tested was absolutely normal. The muscle tests, the reflexes, the atrophied limbs—*everything was perfectly normal!* Then he told us that we should thank God, take all of our money out of the bank, and go on a long vacation! Actually, we did go away two days later to get away from everyone as news of my healing spread. We packed our camper and headed for

North Carolina where we were to meet my parents.

For as long as I live, there is no way that I can ever give enough thanks to the Blessed Mother and to God for all the grace they have given to me and to my family. It may sound strange to say that all that happened to me I believe happened for good, but I sincerely believe that. My spirit is stronger and my faith is deeper. God and the Blessed Mother showered me with their grace, and if that included enduring what my family and I did for so many years, it was worth it. There is no healing so divine as the healing of the soul.

RITA KLAUS
Butler County, Pennsylvania

For Rita Klaus's own account of her miraculous healing, I refer you to her book, Rita's Story, *published by Paraclete Press.*

IN A WORD, my life was a *mess*!

I had been strung out on drugs for fourteen years, and there was no earthly reason for me to even still be alive. I had begun to experiment as a teenager, and by the time I was twenty-six, I had a five-hundred-dollar-a-day cocaine addiction. I was malnourished, my teeth were rotting, my hair was falling out. I was getting black eyes and broken bones mostly as a result of a long series of events that left me out on the street, and with different men.

I could no longer inhale cocaine, because I had burned a hole in the lining of my nose from abusing it. I still needed it though, on a daily basis to function at all, so I started free-basing. Sometimes after smoking it, I would hallucinate. I could feel things moving all over my skin and I thought I was covered with bugs. I felt that I had to get them off me—no matter what—so I ripped open my skin, pulled out my hair. It got so bad that I even mutilated myself with razor blades, tweezers, and scissors.

I had spent time in different treatment centers, but none of them could help me. Eventually my aunt saw me and was convinced I was near death. She had been to Medjugorje in 1988, and begged my mother to let me go back with her. My mother had already given up on me, for some very good reasons, and I had really given up on myself, too. I had no intention of stopping what I was doing, and even if I had wanted to, I wouldn't have known how. My aunt felt that taking me to see the Blessed Mother was my only hope.

I can look back now and see that something was happening to me in spite of myself. Two days before I was to leave on what I thought was a vacation, not a pilgrimage, I just decided that I wasn't going to buy any more drugs. To this day, I don't know why I decided to just use up what I had left and not worry about where or when I'd get more, but that's what I did. I never even took this decision to its logical conclusion, which was that by not buying more drugs I would be entering into my own hellish withdrawal, which would not be smart! But like I said, I wasn't thinking that far ahead, which in itself was miraculous.

After we arrived, I still didn't get that this tiny village was supposed to be a holy place. I saw a lot of praying going on, which kind of turned me off. It took a couple of days to really let it sink in that prayer was *the* activity there. Once again, something came over me to make me willing to give it a try.

I went to confession with an American priest, telling him everything that had brought me to that point. He then blessed my sores with holy water, the sores that I had worn for years and years. By that evening, they were all closed—and within a few short days, they were completely healed! I also had an exorcism. Father Jozo prayed over me, and my aunt made arrangements for me to meet one of the visionaries. Vicka came and blessed me with a prayer to the *Gospa* (Virgin). She put her hands on my head and I felt electricity run through me and a tremendous warmth. I had such a strong sense of well-being, it was unreal. For the first time in my life, I felt like I had been freed. I knew that I was going to be able to have my own life again—and that it was given to me as a gift.

At the end of our ten days, my hair had started to grow back in the bald patches, my wounds were all healed, and what is most amazing of all—I had *no withdrawal whatsoever*.

That was more than six years ago, and I have not been near a drug since!

I spend most of my time these days helping still-suffering addicts. I have been all over the United States, Canada, even Guam, sharing my experiences as an addict. I try to give them hope and let them know that through the grace of God, there is another way.

I could never have imagined my life turning out the way it has. I do not have an explanation for what kind of force was powerful enough to change my life so completely, so instantaneously. I just do not know why I have been given a second chance, but that is exactly what I have.

JILL JENSEN
Winnetka, Illinois

IN THE summer of 1993, a month-long spiritual festival was scheduled to be held in Iceland. I had been invited to teach the basic methods of shamanic journeying, one of my areas of intense study. I'm Finnish by birth, and I was very excited about this trip, because it would be my first visit to Iceland, as well as an opportunity to attend a festival dealing with a subject of great interest to me.

I had been told by the Icelandic host who was organizing and directing the festival that it would be a very sacred gathering during July, held in a mystical spot near a remote glacier mountain that was really an extinct volcano. It was way out in the wilderness, on the peninsula.

I did some studying up on Iceland and learned that it is sometimes called the land of frost and fire because large glaciers are found right next to steaming hot springs, geysers, and volcanoes. Some volcanoes are still active, and over the centuries, more than two hundred have erupted, creating glistening lava fields as they spewed forth. I also learned that there are more hot springs and sulfur-steam areas in Iceland than in any other country in the world. Even the word geyser comes from Iceland's famous hot spring, Geysir, which shoots water two hundred feet in the air.

Iceland is, of course, a very cold country—in Reykjavik, the capital, it rarely gets above fifty degrees and that's in July! My host told me that where the festival was being held would be even colder, the weather so severe there that not even potatoes can grow. A silky kind of mountain grass does, though, making for a powerful landscape since there were practically no trees for miles. Early settlers had to chop them down for firewood and that was in the year 1000. Apparently, successive generations did not reseed, so there are no trees, no foliage, nothing but sky and mountain grass as far as the eye can see. An impressive location for a spiritual gathering!

Several months before I was to leave for the festival I got sick. It was some sort of respiratory condition that the doctors couldn't quite diagnose and it hung on and on, which is really strange because I must tell you that I am usually a very healthy person. I'm also a nurse so I had access to the best medical care, but despite my efforts to get better and the care and attention of two physicians, I not only didn't get better, I became progressively worse.

By June, with the spiritual festival less than a month away, I was desperate to feel well again. One of my doctors thought I might have contracted tuberculosis from the AIDS patients I work with as a hospice volunteer. The other doctor suspected leukemia for some reason, and wanted to have tests run. Talk about a difference of medical opinion. The only thing they agreed on was that I *definitely* should not travel. In other words, they told me, I could forget about going anywhere, let alone a cold country like Iceland.

My disappointment was acute. I had been so looking forward to this trip—to go to this unusual country so different from any other, for a festival of spiritual exploration that meant so much to me. I really was heartsick about not being able to go, and wanted to spend some quiet time in meditation.

In my backyard is a tree that is very sacred to me and it's where I go when I need to have a quiet moment alone. It's a birch tree, which usually wouldn't grow in a midwestern climate because the summers are too hot, but this was a particularly unusual tree! My daughter brought it to me from northern Minnesota where, for the two years that my mother was dying, that tree refused to grow. Even so, my mother insisted that my father continue to prune it, saying, "It will grow. Don't worry, it'll grow." And it did—after she died. It has a wonderful white trunk now that is strong and straight, and I often go out there and sit under it, enjoying the peace it brings me. I don't really need to go to any special place to get answers, but when I am under that tree, I find myself in communication with nature, and I'm often able to see my life more clearly.

On this particular day, I received the message: "Don't worry. You go on ahead with your trip, and while you are there, Mother will heal you." In one of those instantaneous moments of clarity when you have a deep, inner *knowing,* I believed in that message. I told myself that the Mother in question had to be Mother Earth because the land in Iceland is so powerful, but she turned out to be someone entirely different!

When the day of departure came in July, I still had a dry, hacking cough, and was terribly sick on the long plane ride. My condition worsened on the long car trip from Reykjavik to the remote peninsula, so much so that my voice was just about gone and my glands were painfully swollen. I didn't know what I would do since the workshop was to be held outside and in the evening. More than two hundred people would be arriving from all over the world in two days' time and I could barely speak!

Gudren, which means God's word, was our hostess, and she showed us around the remarkable surroundings. It was amazing how the land seemed to fall right into the ocean—there was a sheer two-hundred-foot drop right into the water. The area was also a bird sanctuary, with Arctic terns roosting everywhere. Gudren told us about a lovely fountain at the foothill of the glacier, so we decided to go see it, walking over the rolling hills with their silky grass. After about thirty minutes we came to the fountain. It was a natural fountain, about six feet by three feet, with moss floating on the surface. Above the fountain, on a crevice of grey granite, was a statue of the Virgin Mary. Gudren explained that there was once a bishop who came to Iceland to convert the pagans. It had been a difficult journey: His group had run out of food, they were low on drinking water, and they were exhausted. Things seemed utterly bleak for the bishop and his little flock when they came upon this fountain. Afterward, everything miraculously turned out fine for them. The bishop was so grateful that he blessed the spot and left a small statue, no more than three feet tall, of the Virgin Mary.

As we stood in front of the fountain, I knelt down, filled with an urge to splash in its waters! Then, for no reason at all, I started to cry! It was a special, very poignant moment, and before we left, my friend took a picture of the statue. When the photo was developed later, the little white statue of the Virgin Mary glowed like the sun—she was just brilliant. My friend and I both remembered clearly that when she took the picture, the sun had not been shining.

Back at the encampment, we had graciously been given one of the few small huts, whereas most everyone else who would be coming would be spending the month in tents. When I went to bed that first night, sicker than ever, I was extremely grateful for the rustic comfort of the hut. I really was worse than I had been in months. I could hardly swallow, so I had no idea how I would be able to speak. Worried as I was, I still believed that somehow I would be healed, that the message I had received under the birch tree had been true and right. I took the one and only aspirin I had with me, and my friend rubbed a blue, homeopathic oil on my throat, and sleep took over.

And then the strangest thing happened. I'm not sure what time it was because July in Iceland has almost twenty-four hours of daylight, so there was light streaming in around the edges of the room's darkening shades when I awoke. I could hear the terns outside screeching when suddenly the wall of the hut facing the mountain, where the statue of the Virgin Mary rested, just fell away! I saw the fountain and the statue as clearly as if I was there in front of them with no wall, no distance separating us. Then a light that had been illuminating the statue slipped out from the figure and began to grow larger and larger, until its brilliant light had gathered into the image—a silhouette really—of the Virgin Mary standing right before me. I wanted to sit up and see if the image would stay or fade away, and as I did, she moved closer until she was directly in front of me, but extending from the floor all the way to the ceiling. At the precise moment that I sat up, I sensed that I was well! Not merely better, but well. No swollen glands, no trouble swallowing. Soon the figure began to slowly fade away until there remained only a faint, phosphorescent glow where she had been.

The message I had been given in meditation had come true, and I did have this glorious recovery. When we returned to Chicago, my doctor wanted to see me right away. "No," I told him. "I don't need to come. I'm really well." That didn't satisfy him. "I'm glad you're feeling better, but I still think we should run some tests."

It took a while, but I finally convinced him that I wasn't just better, I was great!

I haven't been sick a day since that encounter with the Virgin Mary, and when I had an opportunity to share my story with Gudren, she wasn't at all surprised. She told me that many sacred ceremonies had been held at the fountain to invoke the presence and the blessing of the Virgin Mary.

On a cold, remote peninsula with terns cackling and land too difficult to farm, the Blessed Mother has her fountain for all those fortunate enough, as I was, to visit there.

PIRKKO MILLER
Oak Forest, Illinois

FIVE YEARS ago, on Martin Luther King Jr.'s holiday, my son was in a terrible automobile accident. He wasn't really expected to live, and if he did, it could be in a vegetative state. He was in a coma, having suffered a broken neck and a punctured lung. Then, to further complicate the situation, he developed pneumonia while in a coma. His doctor told us, "Don't expect any miracles. We think your son has extensive brain damage. The recovery, if there is one, will be very, very slow. It will take a long time before you are going to see any improvement at all."

My son was in the intensive care unit. There was a little room nearby where my husband and I kept vigil since we were not allowed to be with our son constantly. There was a television in this room, but we really couldn't concentrate on any program because we were so worried. Then a show came on about the Blessed Mother, and her appearances in a small town in Yugoslavia. I had never felt particularly close to the Madonna, but I was drawn to that show and as I watched, I felt a great sense of peace fill me, which I certainly did not expect to experience under the circumstances.

After the television program, my husband and I went in to see our son. His eyes fluttered open slightly and I thought I saw him smile at me. I was sure I was imagining this because he was still unconscious, but I did feel a ray of hope that maybe he wasn't totally lost to us.

A few days later, a neighbor brought us some prayer beads that someone she knew had brought back from Medjugorje, the town in Yugoslavia that we had seen on TV. She heard what had happened to our son, and she immediately wanted me to have the prayer beads. Even though I didn't have an active devotion to the Blessed Mother, in times like that you feel so helpless, so I accepted the beads and began to use them. I will forever be grateful that I did! Just like what happened when I was watching that television program, a tremendous peace came over me as I prayed. I had been beside myself with worry, and then I felt that the Blessed Mother had come to help us.

My son came out of the coma in twelve days, and was back home with us in one month. He confounded the doctors by making a full recovery—no brain damage, no lasting effects from the accident. I thank God and the Blessed Mother for that. That sense of peace was a sign from her. She was trying to tell me that everything would be okay. My son had a miraculous recovery, and I firmly believe it happened because Mary heard my prayers and asked God to heal my son.

FLORENCE PLACONA
Staten Island, New York

THERE IS A story of the Madonna that I particularly love. It goes back to the 1600s. It seems that Lake Titicaca, on the border of Bolivia and Peru, suddenly began to rise to overflowing, and was about to flood the surrounding countryside. An image maker from Copacobana had a dream that the Virgin Mary appeared to him and said, "If you make an image of me and face me toward the lake, I'll make it stop rising." In those days, holy images were carved in wood, so the next morning, the man worked feverishly to create La Virgen de la Candelaria, as she came to be known. When she was finished, she was taken out to the lake, and it is said that the waters withdrew.

I have visited her shrine in Copacobana, Bolivia, where every year a magnificent springtime festival is held in her honor. People in Latin America love processions, so each spring they take out a copy of the original figure and she is walked around the village to greet the people in celebration. The original still exists, standing on an elevated pedestal, looking out at the lake from a church window. The people will not move her out of fear that if she ever leaves, the lake will rise again.

I have a few images of La Virgen de la Candelaria on a prayer altar in my bedroom as a reminder of that sacred place, but the Mary I feel most drawn to is the Black Madonna.

When I was thirty-eight, I had a repressed memory surface. I recalled being sexually abused by a boyfriend of my mother's after she and my father had divorced. It is difficult to describe the depth of my depression when these memories surfaced. I was drawn at the time to read about Inanna, a Sumerian goddess who descended into the underworld. Her story deeply affected me, and while I didn't relate it to my own life, I did feel an unusual affinity with her experience. The Book of Inanna is one of the oldest stories ever found in written form, and it is part of the epic of Gilgamesh.

During this period, I was riddled with self-doubt. I thought that if I had hidden these memories of sexual abuse for so long, what else have I hidden? How else have I lied to myself? It put my whole sense of perception in doubt, which really frightened me. It was then that the Black Madonna came into my life and became a truly powerful and significant figure for me.

The Black Madonna knows the part of her nature that is dark. Because she dares to recognize her darkness, she possesses a rare wisdom. That is how I came to connect her with Inanna, who went down into the underworld where she was killed and reborn. When she came back, she had a depth to her that no one else in the upper world had, because they had not experienced what she had. This allegory became particularly meaningful to me in my own emotional and spiritual healing.

In December of 1994, I took an art therapy workshop. The final assignment was for everyone to make a shrine that came out of a sacred place within themselves. I am a gardener, I go to school full time, and I have a son, so even though I had a whole week to do the shrine, it wasn't enough time. I wanted mine to be really ornate and profound, but because I was so busy I wasn't able to gather all the materials I wanted for it. At the last minute I ended up pulling together anything I could find that was lying around the house, like an orthodox cross, flowers, seashells, ribbons, Greek columns, and, as my centerpiece, a postcard of the Black Madonna from Jamaica.

What was intriguing about this picture is that she had scars on her body and on her face, which is really unusual for Mary. A friend explained to me that the scars were from wounds the Goddess of Jamaica suffered at the hand of Christianity.

I felt that, given how much of my life I had spent in a wounded state, creating this shrine with the Black Madonna as the centerpiece seemed particularly appropriate. It then became a symbol of healing for me, and I developed a relationship with her that has become very personal and very powerful. She has taught me to wear the scars of my wounds proudly, because they have made me who I am.

The shrine, which now sits on the prayer alter in my bedroom, has been very empowering for me. The wounds have not disappeared, but the way I see myself has changed. I am now able to embrace my own dark past and consciously choose to live with that knowledge in the light. I can look into the Black Madonna's eyes today, and I don't see her pain anymore, but rather the beauty of her acceptance. The scars are no longer the first thing I notice about her. It is the depth of her wisdom and knowledge that is so special to me.

Through the Black Madonna's interaction in my life, I am finally able to say, "Enough pain, enough wounding. It's over, the hurting is over. I am perfect the way I am, and that doesn't mean I don't make mistakes. It means that in my humanity, even my mistakes are perfect."

I believe this lesson is especially critical so that one can learn to go forward from our mistakes, rather than collapsing under their weight. The light that shines from the Virgin's eyes says to me, "You cannot deny that I exist as a Black Virgin. You cannot deny that the black side of the Virgin is here. I have always been here and I am never going to go away, but if you embrace me, I will heal your scars." And she has, by showing me the beauty of accepting who you are, both dark and light.

CARLA CURIO
Santa Fe, New Mexico

TEN YEARS ago Jesus showed me that I should be in service to God and that I could do this by healing through my hands. Since I was used to being guided by Jesus, his message did not seem unusual. Then about two years later, when I was working on a client at the healing center where I have an office, something truly extraordinary did occur.

I was working on this woman's heart. We were in a small room, and as had happened in the past, I had a vision of Jesus with me. When he had first shown me how to be of service to Our Lord, he had assured me that he would teach me and guide me. Therefore, having a vision of him while I was with a client was not that odd. What was odd is that while my client was on the massage table, I felt hands come over mine as I was deep in meditation.

I looked up to see an incredibly beautiful woman. I didn't recognize her immediately because I was so unprepared, but within seconds her beauty and her white robes with gold belt and gold trim told me who she was. Her hair was dark brown and her eyes were brown as well, and her heart-shaped face was so sweet. There was such goodness and peace there! She smiled as I looked up at her and recognition dawned on me. I knew that Mary was with us as the Mother, and I didn't know what to think because the woman I was working on had recently left her church. I didn't know if she would be receptive to what I was seeing, but I wanted to try—knowing what an incredible blessing it was.

"Open your heart and your mind to receive who is present with us," I said, "because it is such a beautiful gift that we are being given." When I asked her if she saw anything, her answer absolutely amazed me, but I learned a very important lesson from it. She told me that she was seeing an image of a Japanese woman and a tall, Native American chief! There I was gazing at Our Holy Mother and her Son, and this woman is seeing a Japanese and a Native American! I was flabbergasted, to say the least. Then Mary spoke to me, and with a smile of understanding simply said, "We come to people in ways that they are able to relate to. Ultimately what matters is that they turn their hearts to God, and not the form in which we appear." Of course! It didn't matter *what* a person saw; it mattered only that they turn back to God.

In October 1988, I found myself going to Medjugorje when I had absolutely no intention of going there—but believe me, I was led there as surely as I was guided into healing.

I had been receiving an inner calling to go to the site where the Blessed Mother had been appearing since 1981, but I didn't want to go to Yugoslavia so I simply ignored it. Then one day as I was walking down the street, I overheard a woman on a payphone saying, "Oh yes, we're going to make our second trip to Medjugorje." This time I could no longer ignore that it was a sign. I waited for the woman to end her call. I introduced myself and we began to talk—and within five days, my husband and I were booked on a flight to Medjugorje!

To this day, I'm convinced I was the only non-Catholic there. I was so innocent that when I did buy a rosary, I thought I was supposed to wear it around my neck! Despite my ignorance, it was truly a perfect trip. My husband and I huffed and puffed our way to the top of the Hill of Apparitions. I was filled with love and admiration at the sight of so many old and infirm people walking up this mountain to honor Mary.

When we reached the top, I sat down to meditate, and that's when I smelled it. The scent of roses came in a wave over me, an overpowering smell, and I asked my husband if he could smell it, but he didn't. Others around us heard me, though, and then someone said, "That's her essence. The scent of roses means she has come to you."

I felt so tremendously gifted by this experience and when I returned home, my real teachings from Mary began.

I learned about the nurturing of the Divine Mother and how very sacred healing and guiding energy is. We must not squander it, or worse, abuse it. At this particular time in my life, I was far busier than I had any business being. I had a full-time job as a flight attendant, I had my healing practice, and I also facilitated workshops at the Robert Monroe Institute in Faber, Virginia.

I thought I could go on forever, but of course, I couldn't. I came down with a pain in my hip that was so excruciating that I could barely walk, and for the next three months I was bedridden. No one could find anything physically wrong with me, except a severe case of exhaustion. I determined that it was part of the spiritual transformation that was going on inside of me since returning from Medjugorje.

Mary and Jesus continued to appear to me, their love and wisdom so encouraging and comforting that I wanted to get well so that I could continue to serve God. During this period of spiritual gestation, growth and change, I learned some very important lessons: I was taught that I, like all of us, am the love of God, living in this human form for the joy of that experience. Jesus did that—he was able to man-ifest love in form, and that was one of the things he and Mary were here to show us.

Mary is very present on the planet right now, helping people remember who they are and how to live with as much love as they can. We really can have heaven on earth, and we can walk with God as we were originally intended to do. I feel a tremen-dous love for Mary, and she does represent Mother God for me, as Jesus is Father God. They are the parents of this planet, and they are here for everyone—in many forms.

This is really one of the greatest lessons I have learned from them. I once had a vision that I was very deeply connected to Madame Pele, the goddess of fire who created Hawaii. I actually have a birthmark at the base of my spine, on the first *chakra*—the sacred bone—that is the exact shape of the island of Maui, and it is red, which is her color. I believe that Madame Pele is the Mary of the Hawaiian culture, and that Maui, her son, is the Jesus of their culture. Similarly, there is a tradition of the Black Madonna within Christianity, and a black Christ for the Mas'ai people of Africa.

One day I was being treated by a kahuna, and it was a very physical kind of massage therapy. I started to have visions immediately. This therapist had also had a year in training with Native American holy men, so she knew a great deal about their culture and traditions. I described my vision as she worked on me. There was a circle of white rocks with a white teepee in the center. The door of the teepee was facing east. A young woman dressed in white kidskin with fringe came out and began to walk clockwise around the circle. She walked behind the teepee and when she came back around to the other side, she was holding a bundle of white eagle feathers in her arms. She put them down in the southeast part of the circle, and then bent over to ignite them. The smoke filled my vision and I couldn't see anything until a pipe bowl emerged, from the west, with the stem appearing in the east. They were both white, and the bowl seemed to be made of some kind of white jade, while the stem was made of wood. The two parts were coming together, and when they joined, the smoke billowed from the pipe. I told her that the message I felt was that the east and the west would soon unite, and that there shall be peace.

I later learned that the woman I had seen was White Buffalo Calf Woman, so much like Mary— young, ageless, beautiful, and leading her people back to God through prayer and devotion.

I was once meditating on the Native American medicine wheel when I saw Madame Pele and all her fire claim the center of the wheel. Then White Buffalo Calf Woman appeared, and Crystal Woman— then Mary. It was Mary who said, "We are all one. There is no separation. We are the Mother energy of all that is."

They are all here to help, guiding us with heavenly wisdom to a higher love.

SUSAN CORD
Redondo Beach, California

FOR QUITE some time I had been in excruciating pain in my back and legs, especially my knees. The nights in particular were unbearable, the pain so bad I was lucky if I got three hours of sleep. Nothing helped, not the painkillers or sleeping pills. If I walked or if I sat with my legs up, it didn't matter, there was no relief from the constant pain.

After a series of examinations by one specialist after another, it was determined that I would need total knee replacements on both knees. I was also told to start using a cane and to walk with great care. This occured in December 1991, and the orthopedic surgeon scheduled me for surgery after the new year. Before he would operate, though, he wanted me to give blood for my surgery, since he would only use a patient's own blood in the event a transfusion became necessary.

I was not happy about the pending surgery. First of all, I was over seventy years old and twenty years ago, when I was fifty-four, I had a dreadful experience during minor surgery—and the knee replacements were not considered minor. What happened then was that the night before the operation I had a premonition that I would not come back from the operating room. My fear got so bad that the doctor was called in to reassure me, and finally I decided to go ahead with the procedure.

My heart stopped on the operating table. I had an out of body experience which I remember clearly. The doctor later told me that he had quite a time reviving me, and that the experience taught him never to operate again if a patient had a premonition such as I did. All this came back to me as I considered the six-hour knee surgery. I prayed and prayed that somehow a miracle would occur and I would not need to go through with the dreaded procedure.

It was about this time that I heard about the woman, Nancy Fowler, who was speaking to the Blessed Mother every month when she appeared in Conyers, Georgia. I felt so sure that if I were to visit the place where she was appearing, that I would not need the surgery. I just knew this deep down in my worn-out heart. I felt this so strongly that I told people that I'd go ahead and start saving blood for my doctor's sake, but I wasn't going to need it because there wasn't going to be any operation.

I found a travel group that was chartering a bus from Deerfield Beach to Conyers from March twelfth through the fourteenth, and I made a reservation. Then I convinced my doctor to hold off on the surgery until I returned. I was thrilled, too, that the trip was scheduled for March since March 21 is my birthday and I took this to be a very good omen!

The bus was scheduled to leave at seven A.M. and so I awoke early enough to drive from my home in Fort Lauderdale to Deerfield Beach with time to spare. I arrived at St. Amrose Church, the meeting place, at six fifteen, and as the minutes ticked away, not another car or bus showed up! I was heartsick, and so I went into the chapel to pray to the Blessed Mother for guidance.

At exactly seven o'clock, a woman came into the chapel and told me the trip had been canceled! I explained that it was imperative that I be in Conyers the next day, because I was one of the few names chosen to be allowed in the room of the apparitions during the Blessed Virgin's visitation. This woman, Bessie McCoy, was very kind and understanding. She suggested I wait until after the seven thirty mass before doing anything. I prayed so fervently during that mass, asking God to help me get to Conyers.

I not only needed a way to get there, I needed someone to travel with. I asked Bessie but she couldn't, and she introduced me to a lovely lady named Mandy, but she couldn't either. However, Mandy took me to a prayer group in Boca Raton where she thought I might find someone to join me.

There were about twenty people gathered together, praying and reading the scriptures. Mandy introduced me and explained my plight, and one very sweet woman, Denise, was able to pick up and drive with me on the spur of the moment. I was ecstatic!

By ten thirty in the morning, I had been with some of the most beautiful and generous and kind-hearted people I have ever had the privilege of meeting. One woman volunteered to go to AAA in Del Ray for a map and travel directions. Another went off to a local deli to make sure Denise and I ate well before we left. Another supplied sweaters and sweatsuits for Denise because it was cool in Conyers and although she rushed home to pack a small suit-case, she forgot to pack warm clothes.

Finally, shortly after one o'clock in the after-noon, we were on our way! God had certainly heard my prayers to get me to Conyers, and had answered them by providing me with so many new friends!

*   *   *

There were hundreds of cars and slews of buses in the parking lot. Fortunately, my handicapped parking permit enabled Denise and me to park quite close to the visionary's house so I wouldn't have to walk far. We saw that people had come from many states, and there were television and newspaper reporters everywhere.

When I approached the ramp leading up to the house, a man told me to wait because there was some sort of problem, and I couldn't enter the room of the apparitions yet, although it was my scheduled time to do so. I sat down, waiting and watching as many people were politely asked to leave and come back the next month. It turned out that there were thirty-one names on the list of those who could be in the room with Nancy Fowler, and the number could not exceed twenty-three. To be one of such a small group was another of God's blessings to me on this trip.

At five minutes to twelve, the visionary, Nancy Fowler, entered the room. It is so difficult to express what I witnessed, it was so breathtaking. I saw the Blessed Mother descend through the ceiling, floating down into the statue of Our Loving Mother that was at the front of the room. A brilliant white light illuminated the entire statue, and I could feel the Holy Virgin's presence and glory in that room. Tears streamed unchecked down my cheeks, and then it was as if a hot rod pierced my heart, flooding me with this incredible warmth. I knew at that precise instant that I was being healed!

The Blessed Mother remained in that room for

over two hours, and when she ascended back to heaven, I saw the brilliant white light drift upward and then pass right through the ceiling. All around me, in a babel of languages, people were praying their thanks for the blessing they had just received. Truly I have never experienced anything more beautiful in my life.

I returned to Florida on cloud nine—and I've been floating on it ever since! I live totally without pain, without pills, without surgery—and I'm sleeping like a baby again.

Last May, I returned to Conyers in thanksgiving to the Blessed Mother. I decided to leave my cane— which I never used anymore—in testimony to my healing. Have hope and faith in the Blessed Mother, no matter how old you are, no matter how hopeless your situation. I love her so dearly and I wish for others to do so, too.

CARMEL CORRELL
Fort Lauderdale, Florida

JOE

ALTHOUGH I didn't know it at the time, everything really began in July of 1986, during our first night on vacation. We were asleep when I woke suddenly, feeling nauseated. I went to the bathroom, but nothing happened and the nausea left. I attributed it to jet lag, and went back to sleep. The rest of the vacation I felt fine and so I never gave the incident another thought.

In October of that same year we went to Medjugorje, Yugoslavia, a trip we had planned for some months. Same thing: first night, I awoke from sleep nauseous; went to the bathroom, nothing. Once again, Cathy and I told ourselves this was just my body reacting to a long plane ride.

But when the incidents of nausea at night became more frequent after we returned home, there was no way we could continue to attribute it to travel fatigue. Within time, I began to vomit continuously; that's when Cathy and I knew I had to see a doctor. I was examined thoroughly after I told him about the two incidents in Europe and then the escalation of problems back home. Not masking his concern as he probed and palpated my abdomen, he finally advised me to have a CAT scan.

I went in for that test a few days later, and to this day, Cathy and I can hear the words the doctor spoke to us as if it were yesterday and not years ago; they were words we can never, will never forget. "You have an enormous abdominal mass," he said, recommending further testing. Additional tests all came to the same conclusion: I had a tumor nine and a half inches in width and even longer in length.

Shortly after this came Christmas, and it was a remarkable season for Cathy and me and our seven children. Surgery was scheduled for right after the new year, and with the possibility of cancer and its finality everpresent in our minds, our family appreciated the real meaning of the Christmas season more than we ever had before, cherishing the gifts of life and love we shared with each other far more than any material presents.

On January 6, the feast of Little Christmas, the Epiphany, the tumor, which weighed over eight pounds, was surgically removed. It was diagnosed malignant. The possibility of cancer had become reality.

Now many years ago, Cathy and I went on a Marriage Encounter weekend, and since that time, each day we take the time to write down our love for each other and then discuss what we've written. We call it our daily dialogue and part of this dialogue has always included prayer. This is a particularly important part of our marriage tradition, one that has brought us a tremendous amount of peace and comfort. We continued it during my hospital stay, not missing one day of dialogue and prayer time, and it was through this that Cathy and I had the strength to face cancer and what it would mean in our lives. We also decided that I would have no chemical or medical treatment. Love and prayer, we believed, would see us through.

CATHY

NO WORDS CAN adequately describe the time in the hospital during and after Joe's operation. When I was told the tumor was malignant, life seemed to go out of me, plunging me into a pain-wracked hell that left me void of all hope, all feeling. I seemed to be numb, empty, and worst of all, helpless to change anything. During the long, frightening hours by Joe's side, I was always surrounded by loving family and good friends. In a way, this became the deepest and most memorable experience of the church I had ever known. Father Meyer and my friends from church fed me, slept by me, took care of the children, and prayed with and for us. Terrifying as our ordeal was, they gave me the strength to go on. On my darkest day, as I sat at Joe's bedside and prayed, I looked at the crucifix above his head and I asked Jesus to die again, this time just for Joe. As unworthy as this may sound, I believe the days that followed showed me that my prayer was answered.

At one point the surgeon told me he would have to remove every organ the tumor touched, but it turned out that only the tumor itself—at least most of it—had to be removed. One pound of the tumor had to remain in Joe's body because it was abutting his right kidney and also had reached some of his back muscles where removal could risk paralysis. Some had also wrapped itself around the vena cava and aorta, the main artery and vein to the heart. To remove the tumor from these fragile areas could be more dangerous than the tumor itself.

The day after Joe's surgery, when I saw my life as a roller coaster of panic, I received a call from Frank and Nives Jelich in Kansas, who had been our guides on our trip to Medjugorje in the fall. They told me about some holy pictures they had received at Christmas from Marija, one of the Medjugorje visionaries. These pictures had been blessed by the Virgin Mary during one of the apparitions, and the Jelichs sent one to us, which arrived two days later. It was a beautiful picture of Our Lady and Baby Jesus, along with a note telling me that many rosaries were being said on our behalf. The difference in me before I looked upon that picture and after is the difference between hope and defeat.

Life and hope came back to me like the first sunlight of dawn after the darkness of night. I knew my love for Joe was strong enough to dispel all fear, even the fear of cancer. In the days and weeks that followed, the doctor predicted many problems, yet each time one threatened, Joe and I prayed together and the threatened problem would disappear. He escaped infection and high temperature. He had no leakage in a repair the surgeon had made. His blood chemical imbalance ended. Remarkably, Joe came home to me and the children fifteen days after surgery. The doctor called it a marvelous recovery, but he warned us that Joe was not cured and that the cancer would return. "The tumor will grow again," was his prognosis. But I remembered my prayer to Jesus, and I drew strength.

Each day together at home became a divine gift for us. We had a saying in our house: "We put all our eggs in one basket and we give that basket to God." We knew that Jesus has said: "Whatever you ask the Father in my name, he will give you," and "I have come so you may have life and have it to the fullest." These words and our total faith and belief in their promise became our salvation, strengthening us with hope that Jesus could and would prevent the cancer from returning.

One day during Joe's recuperation at home, I remembered something about our trip to Medjugorje. While there, I had worn some special rosary beads around my neck. Two days before we left, we were in the field by St. James Church, practicing songs for our mass in English the next day. It was delightfully warm for October, and so I took off my sweater and beads. I never saw the rosary again. When I remembered this, I found great comfort in the knowledge that an important part of us had been left in such a holy place.

All through this time, we tried to live Mary's message to pray, fast, and say the rosary. Every time I said the rosary, I encountered a vision of Mary, coming to Joe and me across that field in Medjugorje—it was a glorious feeling. We prayed every day, and every night we said the rosary together as a family. We tried, too, during these difficult times, to live Mary's message of hope, and as strong as our spirituality and love for one another and our family had been before Joe's illness, it was richer now, deeper, purer.

For Father's Day, the children gave Joe a candle with a butterfly on it as a symbol of new life. Written on the candle were the words: "Expect Miracles." And we did!

Joe's surgery had been back in January, with a new CAT scan and other tests not scheduled until July to determine where—not whether, but where—the cancer had grown again and what action to take. The week before the scheduled tests was a particularly difficult one for me, despite the recent months of hope and strength and love and prayer. I was emotionally fragile as never before. Joe and I went to a meeting where a slide show was presented with the background theme of "Through the Years" by Kenny Rogers playing, a song that was especially poignant to me with those tests looming.

Joe had asked the doctors that I be allowed to be with him during the CAT scan, and I was glad about this, but it also made me terribly nervous, of course. In the days shortly before the tests, I asked God for a sign that Joe would be cured. As strong as my hope and faith were, I was so frightened that I needed more—and I received it. Later that same day, Joe was resting in the yard and when I came outside, I saw that he was outlined in a glow, as if the sun's rays were falling on him and him alone. It was astonishing, and I knew without a doubt that that was Our Lady's own sign! God had heard my prayer and answered me, and the strength that gave me is indescribable.

The CAT scan was scheduled to begin at ten A.M. Joe and I attended mass first and said the rosary before heading for the hospital. We took communion together, and as we turned to go back to our church seats, an extraordinary thing occurred. Jesus himself came to stand beside me and then spoke to me. "Cathy, when these tests are done on Joe today, it will be my body and my blood that they will see." Never have I known such a swelling rush of joy. Confidence filled me. I felt redeemed and safe, with nothing to fear.

JOE

THERE WERE DAYS waiting for my test results when I wondered if we had done the right thing in deciding to have no medical treatment after my surgery. The doctors had told me there was a possibility that chemotherapy and medication could retard the regrowth of the cancer for a few months, and since then, I admit there were times when the fear of having this cancer running rampant through my body without medication as a defense made me think we were fools. Friends told us that faith and fear cannot coexist, and Cathy and I certainly found this to be true!

One day, however, as I was driving in my car, I suddenly felt a sense of real joy come over me. It was so profound a feeling that I began to smile as I drove. And then, from deep within me, I heard these words: "Don't worry about the results of the scan. It can only be a distraction from what we need to be doing. I will take care of it. We have too much to do to become distracted by this."

In that moment, all kinds of ideas began to flash through my mind about how Cathy and I could reach out to others to enrich their marriages. That is what we were needed for, what we were meant to do.

Cathy and I had made plans earlier in the year to return to Medjugorje, convinced that Our Lady was beckoning to us to go back. We still hadn't heard the results of my test, although several weeks had elapsed since the scan had been taken, and we were scheduled to leave for Yugoslavia the next day. We decided to call the doctor, since it was important for us to know whether our prayers in Medjugorje should be of petition or of thanksgiving.

The doctor said it had taken so long to get the test results back because he had sent them to several other doctors and had been waiting for their opinions. He finally had them all. He told us there were no new tumors on the scan, and there was nothing in the blood tests that was abnormal. And then he said that the pound of tumor he had left in me was gone! There was only one centimeter on my right kidney that appeared as a blur on the CAT scan, that's how small it was.

"It looks like we have a miracle on our hands," I said.

"I'm glad you said that because I didn't want

to," he replied, and when I repeated that it was a miracle, *the doctor*, a man of science and fact, said: "I certainly can't deny that!"

Cathy continues to pray over me every night before we go to sleep. She blesses me with water from Medjugorje and makes the sign of the cross on my abdomen with soil we took back with us. We will never forget that while I was in intensive care after my surgery, the visionary, Marija, took me spiritually into the room with her during an apparition of Mary, asking her to intercede for me, that I might be cured. We will also never forget that during our very first visit to Medjugorje, before we knew of my cancer, we were allowed to go into the room of apparitions and pray there alone—and we prayed that together we might do God's will.

That August of 1987, after we heard the results of the scan, we returned to Medjugorje, this time with our son, Chip, and with our pastor, all of us offering prayers of thanksgiving. In 1988, at Christmas, we sent a card to the priests at St. James in Medjugorje, along with two articles Cathy and I had written for *Matrimony Magazine* about my healing, and the growth in faith we had experienced from the ordeal.

A few months later, we received a letter from Father Slavko Barbaric requesting copies of my medical records and an account of the part we believed Medjugorje had played in my cure. There is a form for the documentation of all possible miracles of Our Lady of Medjugorje, and we filled this out and sent it to him with all the records available to us.

Three years after our original trip, we journeyed back once again. We brought my most recent medical test results to update the records there. We met with Father Barbaric and he looked up my name in a big book. We were listed as case number 353 of "possible" miracles which may someday be attributed to Our Lady. For Cathy and me, there is no "maybe" about it. We will forever be certain that she gave us the gift of a miraculously healed body and a renewed faith in our love and purpose on earth.

JOSEPH AND CATHY ROMANO
Paradise Valley, Arizona

I AM A priest in an exceptionally small Russian Orthodox monastery in New Mexico, so small that monastery is really a misnomer. Technically, we are a "skid," meaning that there are only two or three monks here at any time, as well as two nuns who live nearby. We are almost unknown, except by word of mouth, from those who have visited us, but like all holy houses, we welcome any pilgrim who comes here. And despite what has happened within our modest walls, we shun publicity and any form of notoriety.

Our story goes back to five years ago, when a young monk here died at the age of twenty-four. His was a particularly painful death for me since the young man had been my first convert, the first person I had ever baptized, the first monk, then the first deacon of this tiny parish—and then the first person to die here. It turned out he died of double pneumonia, but before anyone was aware that he had it, he passed out and by the time he got to the hospital, it was too late to save him. This young monk truly had meant a great deal to me and I was deeply disturbed by his death.

Nine days after he died, I came to the monastery with three icons to dedicate in his memory. Two of them were hung up as saints. The third was the Mother of God, Our Lady of Vladimir.

Even as I was hanging up the icons, I was praying to Our Lady. You see, I felt like a failure over the young monk's death. I felt that if I had been quicker or understood his symptoms better—anything that would have made the difference between life and death. But I had been unable to do anything and the sense of failing had weighed heavy on me those past nine days. I prayed to Our Lady for a sign that my young monk had truly entered into heaven and that I should continue as a priest.

Now as I've said, the monastery is exceedingly tiny so when I suddenly began to smell the rich, deep, heady aroma of roses it startled me with its intensity. I looked around, but of course there was not so much as a rose petal in sight. I went back to hanging the icons, removing the plastic in which she had been wrapped to protect her from being scratched or soiled. I wadded up the plastic wrap and tossed it into the bag in which I had carried the icons. Immediately there was a powerful explosion of smell, there's no other way to describe it except as an explosion.

I looked back at Our Lady, startled to realize that she was wet all over! I automatically wiped her with the sleeve of my robe and almost simultaneously came another explosion of aroma, that rich, sweet, unforgettable scent of roses. I was in a daze of confusion. What in the world was going on?

I again turned back to the icon, and my breath caught in my throat. In the center of our tiny church is a chandelier, and its light was illuminating the most extraordinary sight: Our Lady was crying! Two huge tears were coming out of her beautiful eyes, rolling down her lovely face.

I knew at that moment that she had answered my prayers. My young monk had indeed entered the gates of heaven. I should continue my calling as a priest. And what I also realized at that moment was how much Our Lady loved this tiny, Russian Orthodox skid that she started to cry here—and she has not stopped since!

In time, word of Our Lady's tears spread, and as I said, we shun notoriety except as people spread the word of the miracles here to their families and friends. We bless all who come for Our Lady's tears, and there have been many, many healings that have taken place here. A Catholic priest who visited was only one of many skeptics who said that Our Lady would only cry in a large, Catholic church. Even he seemed to forget that she is the Mother of God. She chooses to be where she wants to be!

I told this priest, "Father, I've been here since this icon has been here which is five years now, and I've returned at least two thousand people to your faith. I have not converted them. In fact," I said to him, "it would have been easy to convert them into the Russian Orthodox church because of the working miracles taking place here. But my only job is to make them believe in God. When you see a miracle from God, then God is real and you will believe."

Today everybody knows about Medjugorje. But does everyone know that on the other side of apparition hill one hundred twenty thousand Russian Orthodox had been killed by Roman Catholics in 1925? Think of the coincidence! She is trying to get us all together—to show us that there is no division in heaven—only on earth is there separation between God's children, and we must put that behind us. Everyone is trying to use the Holy Mother as a weapon, but she is a guide to the healing of our hearts!

Over the years, the healings here have been glorious. Why, the very day that she started to weep, a man was instantaneously healed of cancer of the throat by her tears. People of all faiths have come to be blessed. In fact, one Jewish man was healed of allergies that made him virtually a prisoner of his own skin. But then he complained that he could not tell his people that he had been healed in a Russian Orthodox church by the tears of the Mother of God. And I told him what I told that Catholic priest and what I will tell anyone: "She is the Merciful Mother of us all."

NAME WITHHELD BY REQUEST

RELATIONSHIPS

If you follow her guidance, you will not go astray.
If you pray to her, you will not give up hope.
If you think of her, you will not go wrong.
If she upholds you, you will not stumble.
If she protects you, you will not be afraid.
If she leads you, you will reach the goal.

ST. BERNARD

MARY HAS been my Mother in the purest sense of the word. She guides me, teaches me, shows me which direction to take. She also brought me to the most important relationship in my life, and I now know the blessing of a true spiritual partnership.

It was about seven, eight years ago that I really began to feel that my consciousness, my soul, was opening up to the power of Mary. It was then that I became ordained as a minister, and I was involved with an organization in southern California called the Madonna Ministry that particularly honors women, especially healers, and is, of course, centered around the Blessed Mother Mary.

The very day of my ordination, I had a vision upon waking. Mary came to me dressed in a magenta robe that covered her from head to toes. She was absolutely beautiful, and there was this incredible radiance shining forth from under the hood of the robe. She reached forward to offer me the most extraordinary bouquet of roses, each flower a different color, each tied with a different feather. She explained that the feathers were correlated with the winged ones on the planet, and they, in turn, were connected to her through the rose. It was just the most glorious vision, and on the morning of my ordination, too!

There was more to come on this special day. Later that morning while I was in meditation, Jesus came to me. He and Mary stood together, and he was wearing a raw silk suit, rather Indian or Asian in style with a mandarin collar. His hair was long and light-colored, and he had a beard. They were coming to bless me and welcome me.

The ceremony took place outdoors, overlooking the ocean, and as we took our vows to serve Mary, I finally understood why people have this kind of sacred ceremony and how powerful it can be to take a vow for something, or someone, you believe in with all your heart. That's how I felt that day, and when the ceremony was over, I said to my Mother: "Now I am truly ready to get married."

I had been in one place for over forty years, and when I originally came to California it had been with the idea of just staying a few months, perhaps through the ordination at Christmas, but no longer. By January, I understood that I was to stay for a while, but I didn't want to.

My path was not yet clear to me, so I took a three-day silent retreat in my apartment. "God, what is going on?" I prayed. "I'm doing my work, but I'm not happy. I want to know what it is that I am supposed to be doing because there is no joy here and I can't do it without joy. If I am not moving in the right direction, please tell me what it is that you have planned for me."

On the third day the fog appeared in my room. This happened to me only once before. It's like a mist that descends upon me and my surroundings, and I recognize it as the Christ spirit. Within me I heard his voice as he said, "My child, your heart's desire is not being fulfilled and this is what we want for you more than anything else." Mary and Jesus were there, telling me to allow in the love I deserved. My job was to have the partner I needed to support me and rejoice with me for the next stage of my spiritual development.

Well, after the fog ascended again, I just lay on my bed and sobbed, releasing all the grief and pain I had been holding back over a relationship that had recently ended badly. I sobbed, too, from the comfort of being held in my Mother's arms, which I felt so strongly.

Seven days later I met Bruce, who is now my husband.

What's even more glorious is that just as I was

staying in California, even though I didn't want to be there, Bruce had been called back from Alaska to Los Angeles within eight months of my return there, and he didn't know why he had been called back nor did he want to be there. But the Blessed Mother Mary knew that we were meant to be together.

Since neither of us wanted to remain in California, we prayed for guidance to show us where we could settle for our highest good, and it turned out—though it took six months and a last-minute miracle of money—that brought us to Durango, Colorado. Another miracle—and I know that the Queen of Angels was definitely responsible for this one—helped me open an angel store called Angel Station. I had about one hundred dollars left with no idea of how to get into retail, but I just knew it was what I was supposed to do, and eventually, everything fell into place—home, shop, everything! Especially my relationship with Bruce.

He is so truly a partner for me, learning and growing with me spiritually as our relationship shifts and deepens. This is so different from any kind of relationship that I was ever in before. We have established the bonds of a sacred relationship and when your life is filled with spirit, as ours is, everything—sexuality, creativity, your inner self—all change. It used to seem so natural to abuse a relationship by holding back feelings, creating difficult situations out of hurt. But together Bruce and I are finding true communication and commitment, because we are learning about the extraordinary fulfillment which comes from the spirit. Anything else Bruce and I have is frosting on the cake!

SENA ROSE
Durango, Colorado

M O N I C A

I AM FROM the Philippines—a country of Mary maniacs! For instance, many Filipino girls, like myself, are named Maria in honor of the Blessed Virgin. I am Maria Monica, my sister is Maria Victoria, my mother is Maria Conception. We call ourselves by our middle names to avoid confusion!

There have been many apparitions of the Blessed Virgin in the Philippines over the last few years, and it is a very important event. Her appearances are always written up in the magazines, and her messages to different visionaries are printed up, too. Much of our culture is based on the Blessed Virgin, and we have many holy celebrations for her. For instance, the entire month of May is known as the Santa Cruzan celebration, and we have processions through the streets of every city with young ladies and little girls dressed up in their finest. A statue of the Holy Mother is carried in front of the procession and there are prayer vigils that occur. It is a very holy and special time, and very beautiful, too!

October is another special month, which we call the month of the Holy Rosary, during which time people share their statues of the Blessed Virgin with other families. So you can see that tradition and Mary are very important to Filipinos, and even though I have been in the United States since 1984, the richness of this heritage remains with me. Fortunately, I have been blessed with a husband who loves the Virgin as much as I do, and we both feel that she really strengthens our union. Ironically, even though he is Filipino, too, we didn't meet until we were in the United States.

When we married, we both wanted the Virgin Mary to be part of our ceremony, which was to take place on May 23. She had been appearing to a nun in Akita, Japan, and we feel particularly close to Our Lady of Akita—something I will explain later. Our priest permitted us to leave a photograph of a statue of Our Lady of Akita at the altar, which made us very happy during this special ceremony.

Another Filipino marriage tradition is to leave your bouquet at Mary's altar at the church. Gerry and I were married in Sedona, Arizona, and as we approached her altar, we both started to cry, tears of joy that we felt came as confirmation that we are loved by her. It was just a feeling that washed over us, and you think, "Oh, God, I feel so holy!"

*   *   *

I would like to explain why Our Lady of Akita is so important to us. It began in my native country. My mother and her friend, Baby Bernas, are both travel agents. Well, the truth is that they are more like the gentleman farmer who isn't really a farmer—they're travel agents just so they can take trips!

One day in 1991, Baby told my mother that she had heard about Our Lady's apparitions in Akita, Japan, and after my mother did some research to get information on this obscure little town, Baby and her husband went there. While there, she became so enamored of Our Lady of Akita that she commissioned a master wood carver to replicate a statue of her that she would bring to the Philippines.

Instead, the Bishop of Akita himself called Baby to tell her that he wanted to bring the completed statue to Manila personally! It seems the visionary, Sister Agnes, had received a message from the Blessed Virgin regarding this particular statue, that it was not to be for Baby only, but for all the people of the Philippines.

A big ceremony was held in Manila the day she arrived, and before long people were coming from all over to see the wooden replica. It was only about a foot tall and you could actually cradle her in your arms. In keeping with Filipino tradition, Our Lady of Akita was passed from house to house for personal prayer.

Then, in October of that same year, 1991, a spiritual conference was held in Washington, D.C., and

Baby flew there from Manila. The stewardess was so accommodating that she gave the statue her own seat! After Washington, Baby and Our Lady traveled to a retreat house in New Jersey and then to one in the Bronx, New York.

Although Baby and my mother had been friends for over forty years, she and I had never met. But my mother called me to tell me to expect a call from Baby and to put her up in my apartment. She told me nothing more—not even a word about her involvement with the Blessed Virgin! So, naturally, when Baby finally did call, I was annoyed with my mother and I was feeling very put out. I have a very tiny apartment and I didn't know how she'd be able to stay here.

I was on the telephone speaking to my best friend about the situation when call waiting clicked in. It was Baby on the other line. I put her on hold so I could get off the phone with my friend, saying, "I'm so irritated. I don't know what to say to this lady. My mom just assumes I can take her in." Without knowing anything else about the situation, because, of course, I knew nothing else, my friend just blurted out that Baby could stay with her! Soon enough she learned why she surprised herself and me with this unexpected offer.

When Baby arrived with Our Lady, she told us everything, and my husband, my friend, and I set up a small altar in my friend's living room, with candles burning day and night so that our friends could visit and pray to Our Lady of Akita. We bought prayer beads, too, and gave them away to everyone—our friends and then the people they called. We felt so privileged and wanted to share this gift with as many people as we could.

One night, Gerry and my friend and I decided to sleep on the living room floor, at the foot of the statue. We kept the candles burning all night and each of us woke repeatedly with strange dreams. All of us felt that each time we'd wake, the room seemed bathed in a shimmering, brilliant white light. For Gerry, the dream was particularly vivid, and he'd like to tell about it himself.

GERRY

THE BLESSED VIRGIN has been a major part of my life since I was a young boy attending Jesuit school in the Philippines, so I was used to her miracles. On this particular evening, I was lying there, my eyes closed, yet I could still feel this intensely bright light, even with my eyes shut. I knew that Our Lady was with us and I felt tremendously blessed.

I sat up, not knowing quite what to do, and that's when I had this unusual vision. I saw myself in a swamp, walking through the reeds, a travel bag over my shoulder and other people around, too, wearing peasant costumes of Eastern Europe. Everything was clean and bright as we walked along, and then we came to a marshy area where there was a fork in the road up ahead. Some people went left, others right, and I just kept walking. All of a sudden, I realized that I was wading through a pool of blood and the faces of the people around me were lifeless; they were all dead! It was just horrible, and I was very disturbed, not understanding at all what the Blessed Mother was trying to tell me.

And then I found out. A few months later, the war in Bosnia broke out. The scenes on television and in the newspapers were the faces of the dead I had seen in my vision! I understood and prayed for their souls.

Baby returned to New York during Holy Week of 1994, and the timing was so perfect, because I had been going through a difficult period in my life, even forgetting to pray, but when Monica and I met with Baby that Good Friday, Our Lady's presence was so powerful that I felt strengthened. In fact, when Monica and I got home after seeing Baby, I started crying. I was just filled to overflowing with emotion, it's difficult to explain, but being with Baby brought back all my feelings of being in Our Lady's presence. Since coming to the States, and starting my studies, my priorities had changed and I had forgotten how devoted my family had been back in Manila.

It was as if the Blessed Virgin were saying to me, "You have been doing well, but somehow you have forgotten me. I'm here to let you know that I've never left you and you can turn to me." This was a turning point for me in my spiritual life, and I have never forgotten the Holy Virgin or prayer since then.

MONICA

GERRY AND I are interested in all kinds of spiritual thought, and we also believe that the Blessed Virgin is not only for Catholics. I don't think she cares what you are, so long as your heart and soul are open to goodness and faith. Just look at the places she appears—Japan, where less than 10 percent of the population is Christian. And Egypt, a Muslim country; even Africa.

There's another message that Mary has for us that I think is important to remember. There is a small town called Lipa—about two or three hours from Manila by car. Supposedly, a miracle had occurred in the Carmelite convent there in the 1950s, but when the Church sent a representative from Rome to investigate the authenticity of the miracle, he pronounced the whole thing a hoax. This priest did not believe the nun's claim that rose petals were miraculously falling from the ceiling.

Then, in 1990 or 1991, my mother called to say that the miracle was happening again, and the people of Lipa asked that the case be reopened for investigation. It was, and the truth came out that the priest who had declared the miracle a hoax had deliberately lied—he said on record that he did not believe the Blessed Virgin would ever appear to poor little brown-skinned people! Now that the Blessed Virgin has returned to Lipa, she seems to be saying, "I was here before, but you did not believe me!"

And that is the real message of the Blessed

Virgin for us. We don't feel that we need a church to tell us what is authentic. When people flock to the site of an apparition and pray to her, and heed her messages, then she has given us the greatest gift we can have. With faith and trust in her, no one needs approval or sanctions from an outside source. Just listen to your heart—she will be there.

MONICA FRANCISCO AND GERRY BENARES
New York, New York

I BECAME ENGAGED to my husband, Paul, when I was eighteen, despite an extremely stormy courtship —breaking up and then making up. We were very childish, and we really were just kids ourselves, but we did marry when I was twenty.

An incident occurred when we were engaged that foreshadowed the way our marriage would unfold. Paul had broken off the engagement, and I was inconsolable. I was truly bereft. I was so young, but I was sure my life was already over and that I would never have another chance at happiness. I was in my room, lying on the bed crying, when I became aware of this voice speaking to me, in me, in my heart. I knew absolutely that it was the Blessed Mother. I hadn't been thinking of her, of anything actually, because I was so consumed by Paul breaking off with me, but I did not question that she was speaking to me. I had grown up feeling very close to her. In fact, I had a small statue of her in my room, and although it was all chipped, I would not part with it.

The Blessed Mother told me that Paul did love me in his own way, but that he would never, never love me the way I needed to be loved by him. I would never really have him. You would think I would have gotten even more hysterical hearing that, but I was strangely calm; just having her with me, speaking to me telepathically, gave me the sense of peace I needed. I did not want to accept what she was telling me, though, because I thought what she meant was that we would never get married. I learned that's not what she meant at all!

Paul and I were married for nineteen tumultuous years. I loved my husband very much, and I'd like to believe that he loved me too. Nevertheless, there were many separations and break-ups, and his infidelities, which absolutely broke my heart each time. It didn't take long for me to realize what the Virgin Mary had meant and how right she had been. I never did have my husband the way I needed him, nor did I have the kind of marriage I wanted, one that would have meant a lot of his time and attention.

Although Paul worked at a "regular" job, his real love was writing. It was while he was finishing a book about a couple that had gone on a crime spree, finally getting caught in the mountains of Arizona, that my husband died. It was May of 1994, and Paul had gone to Arizona to photograph the area where the couple had been captured. It was the last phase of the book to gather these illustrations, but he never got to finish it because he died in the desert.

Paul was supposed to be in the desert only for a day, and was going to call me when he got back to his hotel room. He told me he would take a swim in the pool and then catch a plane home that evening. I never got the call from him, so I started to phone around, trying to find out what had happened. When the car rental agency in Phoenix told me that he hadn't turned in his car, I knew something was horribly wrong. The police organized a big search party and there were two hundred people out looking for him. An Indian tracker was even called in to help.

The entire time the search was on, I prayed the rosary and I so strongly believed that my prayers would be answered. When the phone rang and it was the lieutenant in charge of the search party, I felt totally hopeful that he had good news. I maintained that faith right up until the time he told me that Paul had been found dead under a bush, probably looking for shade.

There were very dangerous conditions on the day Paul went out. The police told me that around twenty people die each year under similar circumstances. He had water with him, but it wasn't enough. There was also a nice breeze according to the searchers, so it would not have felt as hot as it really was. He got heat stroke and died of dehydration in his sleep. The incident was covered in the newspapers and on television. The media made a really big production of the story on the news for a while.

My life has had to go on, but with increasing difficulty. Paul left me with three teenagers to raise and a lawsuit. The construction company he had is being sued because he owed some money, which he didn't handle as well as he should have, preferring to work on his book, which he really loved. In addition, Paul never made out a will, so my personal assets, as well as the company's, are being taken.

Years ago the Blessed Mother knew how my life with Paul would turn out. I should have listened, but I was young and headstrong—blindly in love with a man who probably did love me, too, but just not in the same way. I know the Virgin Mary has never left me, even though I didn't listen to her. I know she understands about her children's frailties, and I thank God for that.

NAME WITHHELD BY REQUEST

AT THE TIME my spiritual life changed, I had not been to church in twenty years. My love for God had not diminished, but I did not feel comfortable with how people acted in church, for instance when someone would say, "Oh, she's got the same shoes on she had last year," that type of thing. I didn't feel God was being given the respect he deserved, so I withdrew from the church, although not from him.

Then a few years ago, a friend of my mother's went to Conyers, Georgia, and brought back a book about the Blessed Mother's appearances there. The book was in English and I was the only one they knew who spoke both Spanish and English, so I was asked to translate. That's how everything began for me.

The book intrigued me, so much so that I wanted my mother and I to go there and experience Conyers for ourselves. The cost turned out to be too prohibitive for us, and I remember thinking at the time, "Now come on, Maria. You've never let something beat you this fast. There's got to be a way to go!" And inspiration came to me—or rather, was given to me. I figured out that if *I* organize a tour, I'd get a group discount, and that's exactly what happened the first time. I got forty people together, rented a bus, and with my son, Michael, my mother, and a busload of people, we made our way from Leonia, New Jersey, to Conyers, Georgia.

The first thing I was aware of, after driving all night, was that I wasn't tired. I wasn't hungry either. In fact, all my physical needs were gone. And I began to experience the most incredible sense of peace. I also cried, but they weren't normal tears; it was as if an internal faucet had opened up. I just kept crying and crying. I definitely sensed a presence, too, and said repeatedly to my son and to my mother, "I feel she is here. I don't know where exactly, or how, but I know this is authentic."

I should also mention how impressed I was with the gift and information center. It is run entirely on donations so that if you want something and you don't have the money to make a contribution, you can still take what you want. I believed that Conyers had to be of God if people were able to have what they wanted for free. I really believed the Blessed Mother would not want her children deprived of information about her, just because of money!

I could see that the other people on the trip were reacting similarly. Most of them had taken the trip with a certain amount of skepticism, like me, but in just a few days' time, they were already feeling touched by the peace and love surrounding them. On the way home, everyone was asking when we would make another trip, and we decided on June.

The second time I visited Conyers I had the privilege of being permitted into the apparition room, and the only way I can describe what happened to me is that it was like being immersed in a warm, white light. I was totally oblivious to other people being in the room. I couldn't see anything but this welcoming light, and I have no idea how long it lasted because I lost all perspective on time.

When I left Conyers, I felt that Mary had given me a very personal, special message through the visionary, Nancy Fowler. She had actually spoken to the entire crowd, saying, "Some of my children have separated themselves from God." I felt like she was speaking directly to me, so when I got back to New Jersey, I returned to church for the first time in twenty years.

Now, I had brought my teenage son, Michael, with me on both trips. He is a wonderful son, and one truly graced by God.

Together we decided to invite the visionary to come to New Jersey to speak, and to stay in our modest house during her trip. She was scheduled to arrive on July 17, and I was just a bundle of nerves all morning, wanting everything to be perfect for this very special lady. Michael and I had discussed were she should sleep. I thought it should be the best room in the house, which was my bedroom, but Michael believed she would be happier in his room, although it was smaller. He didn't know why he believed this since he had never met her, only seen her from afar in Conyers, but he was insistent about it so I agreed.

As soon as Nancy arrived, she asked for a few minutes alone to pray and headed directly into Michael's room. When she came out, she said she had been told to give us the cross she had been traveling with and that it should be given a place of honor in our home. There was not a moment's thought for me. Since Michael is the biggest thing and the best thing that has ever happened to me, the cross was placed in his room.

He met her for the first time when he came home from school that day. We were in the kitchen, making introductions, and it was strange the way she just kept staring and staring at him. I finally had to ask her what she was seeing because I was so unnerved. I will never forget her answer. She said that Christ was standing behind my son. Michael and I both started to cry. I could see that he was a little bit uncomfortable, but I told him not to fight his feelings.

The next day Nancy had a speaking engagement, and before she left, she had gone into Michael's room to pray. Edwin was a seminarian traveling with her, but at this time, he was in the living room with Michael, my husband, and myself. Now, I should explain something about myself. Before I visited Conyers, I was trouble waiting to happen. I had a hot temper and a short fuse, and a bad habit of sticking my two cents in everywhere, even if it wasn't wanted! Maybe because my focus had become more spiritual, or maybe because the Blessed Mother was patiently guiding me, I wasn't like that as much anymore. So when Nancy suddenly called out, "Come quickly, the Mother of God is appearing in Michael's room!" I did not get up and run into the room like the old Maria would have done. I assumed she just wanted Edwin to join her, so I remained in the living room. But when she called out for all of us, I went tearing into the room.

Nancy was kneeling down. Michael and Edwin moved toward her in the center of the room, and my husband and I went behind them, with a full view of the room. I didn't see anything, but I felt chills all over my body. Suddenly, Michael bowed down, all the way to the floor as if he were prostrating himself.

Then he started to cry. I had never seen him like this. Fifteen-year-old boys just don't act this way over nothing! I tapped him gently on the shoulder and asked if he was seeing the Blessed Mother. He couldn't speak, so he just nodded. That was all it took for me to go berserk. I started shouting, "I love you, Blessed Mother! I love you!" That was all I could think to say because that was what was in my heart.

And then the most beautiful thing happened. A golden glow surrounded my son, running from his shoulder, all around his head, down to his other shoulder. The same light graced Nancy and Edwin, so I knew they all were seeing her. I was transfixed for what seemed like several minutes, although Michael believes it lasted only a few seconds. I understand that, because no matter how long it is, an experience like that is so extraordinary that you think it could never last long enough.

I continue to go to Conyers on the thirteenth of each month for the apparition of the Blessed Mother, and every time, I am overwhelmed by the miracle of having her in my life. I feel that she and God want me there, want me to continue to bring people there, which I do. And the means to make the monthly trips always comes through because I have learned to trust and accept God's will.

I do regret having been away from church for so long, but I understand now that nothing happens that is not meant to be. I used my free will to leave the church, and now I've used that same free will to return to both church and God in a way that is far more meaningful than it ever was before.

The joy of having my faith restored is one of the many gifts the Blessed Mother has given me. Another is the strength and closeness that my son and I share. I feel that I went to Conyers and returned to the church, opening my heart to God again, with far more trust, for Michael. My gifts are also for him, to support him in the experiences he is yet to have. My son has been touched by the Blessed Mother—there can be nothing more glorious for me than that.

MARIA BEDOYA
Leonia, New Jersey

I'VE BEEN to Conyers, Georgia, several times with my mother. The first time I went as a typical teenager who didn't want to be there so much, didn't know why I was there. I just didn't really believe anything special would happen. I think I was acting like most teenagers would!

That first time, nothing much did happen, except for a very strong sense of peace I felt inside of me. I had never experienced anything like it before and it felt really good.

The second time we went, my mother was allowed into the room of apparitions. I spent a lot of my time worrying about my father, who was scheduled to be operated on for a tumor close to his voice box that the doctor thought might be cancerous. I prayed to the Blessed Mother to please let it be anything but that, but if it was, I asked her to give my family the strength to cope with it and to not fall apart.

My father was going to be operated on the day we were getting back, and while he was in the operating room, my grandmother and I prayed on the telephone together the whole time. He came out of that operation just fine, and it turned out that the tumor was not cancerous. I was so happy that I decided to pray my thanks to the Blessed Mother, who had answered my prayers to let my father be all right.

That was the beginning for me. Since then, I always tell people that if they pray for something and it happens, they should also remember to take the time to pray thanks.

I also tell people that their prayers should be from the heart. If they're not, there won't be any real meaning to them, and I don't believe that God can hear empty prayers.

When the visionary, Nancy Fowler, came to visit us in our home, it became a really incredible experience for me. My mom already told you about what happened in my bedroom, and as soon as I walked in there and saw her praying, my whole body started to tingle. It was unlike anything I had ever felt and it was a sign to me that the Blessed Mother was truly there, in my room.

I prayed silently that I might see her, too. When I looked up, there she was, in the corner, dressed in black! I cannot tell you the feelings I had, seeing her as clearly as I was seeing Nancy or my mother. She was completely three-dimensional, except that her face wasn't clear. There was so much light blinding me that I could only see the oval outline of her face, but I couldn't really make out her features.

I was overwhelmed and felt that I should bow down and just say thank you. Ever since then, I've become very devoted to her and to prayer. Nothing is more important to me. It's gotten to the point that if my favorite basketball player was on his way to my house for a round of one-on-one, I'd have to ask him to wait until I finished praying first!

My sense of priorities in life has changed since that day, too. I used to think only about making money, getting a job to help me pay for a great stereo system, that kind of thing. Now I know that spiritual gifts are the greatest kind of all, and they can't be bought. Like I couldn't have asked my stereo to please cure my father or to please help me with my feelings. The only one who can do that is God.

I have been really touched by the Blessed Mother, and several people who know what has happened to me have asked me to pray for their sons or daughters. Each time I have, they've come back to tell me that they did see some kind of change in their children afterward. I think this might be a special gift the Blessed Mother has given me, and I know it should not be abused by asking for things like passing a test which I haven't studied for! When I ask her for something important, there are usually good results and I always thank her later.

I also go out and talk to other teenagers about my experiences because I think it's important for younger people to get in touch with their spirituality.

Another time I saw the Blessed Mother again, in Conyers. I was in the room of apparitions and my mother was sitting behind me when I felt that familiar chill tingling all over my body. "She's here, I know she's here," I said. "I can feel her again." And then I saw this violet mass that was like a mist forming in front of the room, near the statue of the Blessed Mother. There were thousands of little points of light dancing everywhere, like fireflies. I focused my eyes, and that's when I realized that the dancing lights were really tiny angels flying all over the room! These little cherubs were zipping and darting all about, and I knew that Mary would be there soon because I've heard that angels escort her from heaven.

Mary did come, holding the Baby Jesus. I could just see her veil because she was looking down at her child. When she looked up, I could see everything, every feature. She was so happy, cuddling her baby as she brought him close to her face like she was kissing him. I was so happy to be able to see her again, so afterward, after she had ascended back to heaven, I prayed my thanks to her with a lot of love in my heart.

The Blessed Mother has given me so much, and has a lot to give to everyone. I just think it's important to let her know we appreciate her and to say thank you for everything she does.

MICHAEL BEDOYA
Leonia, New Jersey

AFTER THIRTEEN years of marriage, I had to admit things were not working. My husband and I decided to separate. This was an extremely painful and upsetting time for me, and I sought guidance to help me sort out the confusion I was feeling over the situation. I had heard of a deeply spiritual woman, named Mary, who did counseling and spiritual readings for people in need. I made an appointment to see her.

My appointment was set for August 15, which is the anniversary of the feast day of Mother Mary's assumption. During her reading, I began to sense a very strong presence in the room and felt I needed to say something about it. Before I could, Mary said to me: "I want to share something with you. Mother Mary has been here with us and everything that I have just told you came through me from her."

I was utterly overwhelmed by these words and felt we should do something that turned out to be very Catholic, to honor and acknowledge the grace she was giving me. We knelt at a little altar Mary had made for Mother Mary. It was simple, but lovely, on a green wicker table. There was a small, round incense holder that Mary later gave me to start my own altar. There was also a postcard picture of Christ on the table.

As we lit a candle and began to pray, I felt so safe, so protected; all the grief and confusion about my separation and possible divorce seemed to be washed away in a very emotional release. When our prayers ended, I felt strong and cleansed by the energy and love Mother Mary visited upon me.

Although I didn't know it at the time I made the appointment, I learned soon after that the woman, Mary, whom I went to for the reading was known for having a very special and deep connection with Mother Mary. As I reflected on all that was said, and on the presence of Mother Mary, I began to realize how unusual, and how meaningful, it was that I had picked this particular Mary from so many people who did that kind of work. And that Mother Mary had graced me on August 15, such a holy day! All these connections became a very powerful message for me.

I changed my life radically. I quit my job in corporate management. I went through with the divorce. And I really began to focus on freeing my own intuitive abilities. I believe that we all have this same capacity, but life has a way of getting us to either ignore or shut down that part of ourselves.

*   *   *

I eventually began to do my own readings for people, and after a few months, Mother Mary visited me again. She has been there for three women that I have worked with, all of whom really needed a mother figure to provide the warmth and nurturing that had been missing in their lives.

The first client she came for was a woman who had been abandoned by her natural mother. Mother Mary said to me, "Feel my arms around you both. Feel me holding you in my embrace. Let her know I am here." As I spoke, the woman burst into tears, sobbing uncontrollably, from the power of Mother Mary's presence.

The second time was for a woman who had been adopted and spent years searching for her natural mother. When she finally found her, she was devastated to be turned away by her yet again.

The third instance was somewhat different in that the woman was a lesbian who had been raised in a very devout and strict Catholic family. She had terrific guilt about her sexuality, and Mother Mary asked me to reassure her that, of course, she would not be turned away—that she was accepted and loved.

I still see these three women from time to time, and they have come to trust and believe in Mother Mary's grace. They may not think about her consciously every day, but they know that if they need her, they can call for her in prayer.

As for me, it seems my need for Mother Mary's

guidance has never been greater. I've been divorced for a few years now, and even though I know I made the right decision for me, it hasn't been easy. My intuitive abilities enable me to see to the core of a person, which is always beautiful, but then I ignore or forgive the reality of their present personality. This can be a real problem in dating! And like most daughters, I don't always listen to the wisdom of my Mother!

I once sought Mary's guidance regarding one particular man I was involved with. She came to me as I was in meditation, standing in front of me in her white robes and blue veil, looking so soft and luminous that I was simply awestruck. I asked her if this was the right man for me—which I was sure he was—and when she shook her head no, I was dumbfounded. What was even worse, I convinced myself that this one time, Mother Mary had to be wrong! Let me just say that she was completely right, and I only wish that I had listened to her in the beginning.

It only took one time of going against her advice for me to learn that I will never do that again. I will no longer question her wisdom, and she has become a trusted counselor who always leads me in the right direction.

VALERIE BLAKE
Minneapolis, Minnesota

I HAVE SIX children, four of them adopted. As a family, we have suffered from severe dysfunction, including gambling, drug addiction, and incest. It is very difficult for me to talk about, but my adoptive daughter had to be removed from our home. It even became necessary to have my husband arrested, that's how horrendous things got.

In order for my family to survive, I had no choice but to divorce my husband, which I did legally five years ago. Despite the difficulty of my own marriage, I feel very strongly that people should be connected, that marriage and love are a gift and a blessing. So in this regard, I set up a network of social opportunities for singles and began writing a monthly newsletter. I always include a little spiritual note at the end because I think it's important for people not to forget their love of God when they find love for each other.

I've been doing this for a few years now, and I really enjoy it. I even plan nine public dances a year and one picnic, and people of all faiths and ages come to these events. At the end of every dance, we all gather together in a circle and sing "Let There Be Peace on Earth," and for those few moments, there is! I love it. I recently read a book about God's gifts, that he uses our individual personalities and our life's circumstances as a springboard to serve him in practical, everyday ways. Therefore, if you feel a passion about something, it is probably your calling and this may sound silly, but I'm passionate about my activities for singles!

Last New Year's Eve I attended a Lutheran retreat and there was a discussion about the importance of the Lord's washing of the feet, and what that might mean in our lives today. A young minister got up and said, "The way I see it is that you need to know where you came from. You need to know where you're going. And in the meantime, as one old minister once told me, you pick up a towel and you wash feet."

I then leaned over to my friend and said, "Well, helping feet to dance, isn't that close?" I said it as a joke, but I felt oddly confirmed that in my own little way, what I was passionate about was the right thing for me to be doing in my life. And later during this same retreat, another man began to talk about reflexology and foot massage as a healing for the whole body. This, too, confirmed that my gentle calling, though not as grand as curing disease or establishing world peace, was good and needed. I've even won a Woman of the Year Award for my efforts to give single people a place to come home to, if you will, where they can feel supported and not be alone, and have fun, too. I am proud of the award and of what I am doing to help eliminate a little loneliness in people's lives.

Of course, my children have been affected by

the kind of dysfunctional atmosphere they grew up in, particularly my daughters. My younger birth daughter has become a classic case of acting out by having married a man who sexually abused her. They're now divorced and she's living with another man, but I am very sad for her and how her life is going, even though I understand why.

My oldest birth daughter has found inspiration and strength from the Blessed Virgin and has created a wonderful and loving environment for her young family. Although she left before the situation at home reached its worse, she still suffered immense family brokenness, and yet she was able to overcome that. It is the miracle of her faith that gave her the strength to survive and choose peace. I am so proud of her!

I know my story is not a big, transformational experience where one moment changed my life forever. Rather, it's been a gradual process of rebuilding my life from some very devastating circumstances to the point where I can now bring a little joy to others. I had to fall on my knees before I could learn to open my heart and reach out—a hard, painful lesson that I will never forget.

MARIANNE PICKHINKE
Storm Lake, Iowa

I CERTAINLY HAVE a wonderful mother, don't I? She's really something else and I think she is right in calling my life a miracle. Even though my family had very difficult circumstances to face, I consider myself to be so blessed with a mother like mine and a wonderful husband who shares my spiritual values.

After graduating from college, I was an air force officer for four years, as a program manager and finance manager. My husband, Mike, is an air force officer, too, and we met on our first assignment in Dayton, Ohio, and then married in the fall of 1991.

When I got pregnant we had just moved to Idaho, and not knowing any of the doctors or whom to ask for a recommendation, I went to the most convenient physician, thinking that is what anybody else would do. I started going to him for my monthly check-ups, and invariably, every time I left his office there would be this knot of tension in my stomach. I didn't realize it at the time, but my body was telling me this man was not meant to deliver my baby. Of course, I dismissed my intuition as a case of nerves.

I read *everything* I could get my hands on about child birthing, as did my husband, and after six months we realized that the doctor's philosophy was just not compatible with ours. I firmly wanted to give birth the way God designed a woman's body to function for the role. Eventually, my husband and I decided to find another doctor who was more accepting of our beliefs.

Well, easier said than done, and this is where I am convinced that God showed us the way. A woman loaned me a book about home birthing by Sheila Kissinger, and as I read it, and saw the beautiful photographs of home births, I became more open to the idea. In time, I knew this was what I wanted, and my husband totally agreed.

Giving birth became a truly holy experience for us. Although my mother couldn't be there, a woman named Mary Smith was, and she stayed in the kitchen and prayed the entire time—and it was a long time. I was in labor for twenty-six hours, and throughout, I felt that the Blessed Virgin was there, helping us. The midwife and her assistant were there for the last eight hours of the labor, and my son Jacob was born two minutes after midnight, on July 4, 1994—the same birthday as my adoptive brother, Adam!

In addition to the Blessed Virgin helping us, I know that St. Gerard was definitely a part of our birth. He is the patron saint of mothers, and we began praying to him before Jacob had even been conceived, and we think he was really there for us all throughout our conception, pregnancy, and delivery.

When we decided to have a home birth, I did think about Mary having had a similar experience with Jesus, with a cave birth.

I feel our decision to leave that doctor and do things in a natural way was so right for us and for our son. We also believe it will be right for us again in the future, if we are blessed with another pregnancy.

We have decided against taking Jacob to any of the well baby checks and do not want to have him vaccinated. My midwife, as well as a woman I knew in Ohio, who taught Mike and me about family planning and who has a degree in pharmacology, helped influence me in this decision, but we did our own reading and research before we were sure. We decided not to have Jacob circumcised either, even though he has a Jewish name!

I am convinced that Mary is there for us when we make these unorthodox decisions. There's so much fear in our culture if you go against tradition, and it's so easy for others to label you irresponsible, wrong.

I've turned to Mary often and said, "I know you brought me here to this place, on my journey of mothering, and that you have brought all these people into my life. There must be a reason for it, so please help me to make the right decisions and to be a good mother." The Blessed Virgin has always been a big part of my prayer life, but I have come to rely on her even more since becoming a mother myself. Who would know better than she how to tend to one's children?

Last year we moved to Utah, and after we settled in, I really felt a need for fellowship with other mothers. I found the Holy Family Parish in a neighboring town where the Mom's Groups would meet. Several wonderful things have happened since I started going there, the first being an encounter with a very special woman. I had stepped outside from one of our meetings to nurse Jacob. I was by the chapel when this elderly woman approached me. She was really quite old, with silver hair and a European accent, and there was a truly saintly aura about her. She placed her hand on me and then on my baby, and instantly I felt a tingling sensation travel through my body. I knew that the Holy Spirit was flowing through my child and me, and I felt so blessed by this woman and this powerful experience.

One of the other mothers in the group has introduced me to the Apostolate of Holy Motherhood, and I am very drawn to it. There is a visionary who calls herself Maria Monte, which means something like Adoring Mary. She's a mother of two or three young children, including an infant. She began to have daily visions of the Blessed Virgin and the Christ Child, and started to write down what they told her. Once in a while, her baby would interrupt her prayer time, and the Blessed Mother would say, "Go tend to your child. That is more important. We can do this later!" She has compiled everything they've said to her in a book, and I am just overwhelmed by the idea of being visited daily by the Virgin Mary—what a blessing and miracle. Yet she would understand that my child was even more important than her messages. Incredible!

In her writings, Maria has been told by the Blessed Virgin to form a group of mothers who can change our society by mothering with total love, rather than by protesting against what we feel is wrong. By giving a child such total love and support, they can go out into the world from a place of deep, inner peace and strength—and I love that idea!

Through the Blessed Mother's messages to her visionary here in Utah, I have come to understand what an important and blessed gift it is to be a mother. I have never been more appreciative or understanding of all my own mother has gone through. And with the Blessed Virgin as my inspiration and guide in this new phase of my life, I just hope that she will help me become a wise and loving parent, too.

DENISE, MIKE, AND JACOB TERNEUS
Layton, Utah

DEATH
AND DYING

She has put on the chasuble of the sun, and her
    stole of stars,
and she takes the horns of the slender moon for
    her candelabrum,
And she walks in the way of the Light of the
    world,
the sick lie in wait for her passing,
For she brings our daily bread and the oil that
    anoints all fevered foreheads.

The balm of all pierced hearts and the chrism
    for all our fears,
And she bears sweet charities like a seamless
    garment,
Full of lilies of the field and of five-for-a-
    farthing sparrows,
Down forbidden alleys and over flat hills by
    paths forgotten,
And the urn of living water by which death is
    immortality,
Closing eyes like the eyes of Joseph:

Jesus, Mary, and Joseph, assist me in my last
   agony,
May I breathe forth my soul in peace, with you.
                                        FRANCIS BURKE

WE ALL KNOW that some day we shall die. For most of us, that certainty lies in the far distant future. But for me, I have been confronted with the reality of death. I have learned what it means to die, and I have learned that it is not something to fear.

In 1994 I was diagnosed with breast cancer, and it spread to my lymph nodes. I was only thirty-nine years old, and I had an eleven-year-old son. He lives with me, and I am the one who takes care of him. All I could think of when the doctor told me was, "Hey, wait a minute! I've still got this life to lead and I don't want to leave my son behind!"

A bone-marrow transplant was recommended, and I agreed. For seventeen days I lay in isolation at Jackson Memorial Hospital in Florida. What happened during this stay forever changed my view of life—because I was fortunate enough to experience death.

I was extremely sick, and the only thing I can remember of those seventeen days is this one quiet afternoon. I was alone in my room, and although I was not technically pronounced dead—and my body functions did not shut down—everything in me said that I was dying. I felt myself ascending, moving toward a white light. As I rose, I saw my son on a thick, heavy cord, an anchor rope, and I reached out to take him with me.

I saw white doves fluttering and cooing, and I knew that we were going to heaven. This knowledge filled me with the most incredible sense of peacefulness, of gratification, of glory. I felt absolutely glorified that I was having this experience. I welcomed it with open arms. I reached out to embrace it; I grabbed it and I latched on to it.

As we ascended past the doves, they turned into bright white lights. Everything was in such harmony, and I was filled with serenity and a sense of wonder. I felt so alive—more alive than I had been even before my sickness. I was dying, and it was absolutely glorious.

I would have to say that I was more accepting of the experience of dying than I have ever been of anything that has ever happened to me in my entire life.

We kept rising, and then I saw the silhouette of the Blessed Mother, with Jesus and Joseph. I believe in the Holy Family and upon seeing them, I said, "I'm here to be accepted into your kingdom." The Blessed Mother wore a pale robe and a long veil. Her skin was very beautiful, luminous even, and she looked so youthful. Jesus was in his early thirties and he had warm, loving eyes and long, light brown hair. He was the one who spoke to me, saying, "No, Betsy, you have to go back. It's not your time." I insisted, "Yes, it is my time! I feel very strongly about this. I want to be here!"

Who was I to argue with them, really? I was disappointed, but I also knew that there must have been a reason for me to return to my body. I descended very, very slowly back into my bed. I didn't want to open my eyes so I just peeked through a little bit. I had the sensation that I was not alone. I felt that the bright, white light was still in the room. It was like the sun shining, only brighter. It was such a compelling light—warm and gratifying, enveloping me, and I wanted to hold on to that love so badly.

I realized later that I had not been accepted into heaven yet because I had my son with me. Perhaps it had really been my time, but it hadn't been his. I also understood that the Holy Family did not want me to die yet, but given the choice I would definitely have stayed!

A year later, at Christmas time, I learned that my cancer had spread to my spine and into my brain. I thought, "All right—*now* it's my time, but without my son."

I was immediately hospitalized, with one treatment after another that left me so sick. The spinal taps, the radiation, the chemo—I even had a catheter in my brain for the chemo to drip through. I was such a mess physically that I decided to stop all treatment. It was just too torturous for me to continue. Whatever time is left for me, I want to live with quality of life.

I was very accepting of what the doctor told me, because I trust that my life is in God's hands.

Anyway, one day I said to the doctor, "I want a time. If I stop treatment, how long are you going to give me to live?"

"I can't give you a time," he told me.

"I need something to tell my son. Please, give me an approximate time."

"Okay, here's something for you," he said, "You're on God's time!"

My son is twelve now and he has been so wonderful. I have been able to show him no fear of death, or dying, or of God's will. Since my experience with death, I have never cried for myself or felt sorry for myself. I have never had a pity party—and my son has learned from seeing that.

My doctors have been tremendously supportive, too. People always say to think positive, but I say you've got to think spiritual because that's the only place where true healing comes from!

I don't pray formally every day, because I don't believe that we have to. When we let the light of God's love flow freely through us, it's not necessary to pray the rosary every day. I've taught my son about God's love and how it has been with me constantly since that experience in the hospital. Since I don't blame God for what has happened to me, he doesn't either—and that is very important to me.

I also go to support groups for women who have cancer, to share my experiences. I do this because they are all so afraid of dying and I can tell them it's beautiful! "Whatever your higher power is, accept it, and know you are going on to another world. Don't be frightened by that! The transition is so easy, so beautiful."

That acceptance has been such an important part of my life. It has enabled my son and me to face every day with a sense of joy, and love, and easy surrender to whatever our future may bring.

Of course, dying is a very individual experience. There are hundreds of millions of people on this earth and we are all going to die. I believe we are all going to the same place, too, but how we get there is different. We all have our own perspective of how we perceive God, and for me it is Jesus and Mary and Joseph. When you get there, you won't believe how powerful God's love really is. It's incomprehensible and it has given me the strength to return to life with peace in my heart.

My surgeon looked at me very seriously one day and said, "Betsy, I have told hundreds of patients that their cancer is terminal, and every one of them broke down in front of me. You are the only one, the single one, who didn't. What's your secret?"

"No secret," I answered. I just looked up to heaven.

He nodded with understanding and said, "May God Bless You." He spoke those words with such strength and sincerity that for the first time, tears came to my eyes in his office.

I also have the support of my guardian angel. I used to think that my grandparents and my best friend, who died in a car accident a few years ago, were my guardian angels. Maybe they do watch over me, but there is someone else I haven't known who came to me in a dream. She is very young, not more than sixteen or eighteen, with short, curly brown hair. Her cheeks are so rosy and she has big white wings. She was behind a field-stone fence out in the country somewhere, peeking over at me and giggling as young girls do. She was absolutely adorable, and I found it interesting that there was a divider between us. It left me with the impression that we couldn't be together yet, but she wanted me to know that she was watching and waiting for me.

Right now I don't know what is going to happen. I don't know if God has a plan for me here. I've recently seen three doctors who each said that I was doing amazingly well since I have stopped the treatments. My MRI even came out remarkably improved and I feel okay. If there is something more for me to do here on earth, that's great, although I'm not yet sure what that might be. Maybe it's to reach that one person who is suffering and needs my reassurance. Or maybe it has something to do with my son—to nurture him a little while longer and help him to continue to grow more, spiritually.

And if I'm supposed to be in heaven soon, that's okay too. There are no secrets between my son and me. I always tell him everything that is going on with my cancer. We talk about the possibility of my dying, and we talk about the chance I have to get better by the grace of God.

We have three bottles of holy water from Lourdes, and every night I bless myself with it. I put it down my spine and across the part of my brain that has the cancer. My son blesses himself with it too. This is something that we can share every day.

As ironic as it seems, it is through death that I have learned so much about living. And the most amazing gift I have is the relationship with my son. Instead of tears and anguish and being angry at God, we have used my cancer to deepen our faith. We are a mother and son who share a truly spiritual relationship—a relationship that has strengthened and saved us both.

No matter where I may be, my love will live with him forever.

BETSY PESCHL
Boca Raton, Florida

Betsy Peschl died on Saturday, April 22, 1995.

A FEW YEARS ago, I noticed that my husband, Jacques, a professional maitre d' at some of the most exclusive French restaurants in New York City and Paris, began to lose weight, too much weight and too quickly. He developed sores in his mouth, and was constantly fatigued, which was very unlike him.

Jacques and I were in our fifties at the time, and we were planning to go to France and work for a little while before retiring. Jacques was from Brittany, and we had spent a lot of time with his family in Nice and Cannes. We had our plane tickets. We were ready to go. But I wanted him to go to the doctor first.

In 1982 my husband had been severely mugged and robbed in New York. He had been viciously beaten with a baseball bat, and his leg was crushed. He was taken to a hospital emergency room and operated on. Fourteen pins had to be put in his leg, and during the surgery, it became necessary for him to have a blood transfusion. This was in 1982 when hospitals did not routinely test their blood supplies.

The blood was contaminated.

My husband contracted AIDS. And I am HIV positive.

He died on December 4, 1994.

My husband wasn't very religious, so I had to work hard to comfort him, strengthen him, to make his death easier.

For many months, Jacques didn't want to go to Europe anymore. He was too ashamed to tell his family he had this terrible disease, but in late summer of 1994, we went. He knew how important it was for me to go to Medjugorje, where the Blessed Mother had been appearing. He was so sick at that point we had to take him in a wheelchair, but he went for me. His family came with us to Yugoslavia in September, and everyone knew that I wasn't going for a cure to our condition. I just wanted a spiritual healing so that I could be at peace with everything that was happening to us, to face our death without so much fear.

One day, I happened to look up on our way to St. James Church, and I saw a cross in the sky. It was formed by a cloud, and it struck me as interesting, but it didn't mean a tremendous amount to me. Then later, when we were having a service outdoors, under the Hill of Apparitions, I saw another cloud. This one was shaped exactly like the Blessed Mother. I could see her face, her arms, her hands, perfectly. It reassured me that she was definitely there, that she knew why I had come.

Three months later Jacques died. He died a terrible death, until the end, which was oddly peaceful. He just kind of drifted off in a half sleep, which I was so grateful for after all the suffering.

I am not so much afraid of death itself because I have read so much about near-death experiences, but I do fear the dying. I definitely believe in an afterlife though. Jacques died right here in our home, and I learned a lot from that: one minute he was breathing and the next I felt him actually die. There was nothing left in his bed after that— *Nothing!* And that's impossible for something to be there and then just disappear into thin air. His personality, his being, went somewhere.

I have been to a workshop with Raymond Moody and George Anderson on death and dying. My family, friends—even the nuns who come from the hospice—all encouraged me to go. There is a book written about George called *We Don't Die*, and through him, Jacques was able to reach out and communicate with me. He assured me there was nothing to fear. He said that when I get over to the other side, I will know why we had this terrible disease, but for now I have to keep on living. Jacques told me that I will pass in my sleep, and when I do, he will be there waiting for me.

It is said that when you die, someone is always there to greet you, to introduce you to that other plane where you are going to be. Towards the very end for Jacques, he whispered to me, "I'm sorry to end like this, because we had so many plans ..." "It's okay," I said, "You're ready to go and Mother is waiting for you." He loved my mother very much and he died on her birthday. I believe she was calling him, that it was her birthday wish.

I know the Blessed Mother has been with me, easing my anxiety, preparing me for what is to come. I have been to see her now in Medjugorje and in Lourdes, too, but I didn't need to make those trips to feel her presence. She's right here with me, in my bedroom.

There is so much she can teach us, so much we need to learn. We really have to work at spiritual learning, to be more open. We must learn to pay attention to the coincidences in our lives, find out what they mean, what God is trying to tell us. It's exciting and I have been surprised that more people weren't interested in spiritual things before. Now they are. People are very curious about these things. They want to learn more and it's very enlightening.

I just hope there is a France in heaven. I love that country and I know that's where Jacques would want to be.

DENYSE AUFFRET
East Rockaway, New York

TWO YEARS ago, on Sunday, January 3, 1993, my two grown daughters (ages twenty and twenty-four), a friend of my younger daughter, and a friend of mine, made plans to go on a pilgrimage. We wanted to go to Marlboro, New Jersey, where Our Lady is said to have appeared repeatedly to a man named Joseph Januszkiewicz. We ended up setting off later than we had expected because my daughter, Mary Jo, is a nurse at New Rochelle Hospital in Westchester and her shift didn't end until six o'clock. I was concerned that we wouldn't make it to the apparition site in time to see Our Lady. I became even more concerned when we saw that virtually every street to Mr. Januszkiewicz's house had NO PARKING signs posted. Mary's appearances here had become so well known that the town even had police sergeants posted in the neighborhood, directing traffic to a parking lot in town that was two miles away!

We walked quickly in the forty-degree weather, and the cold bothered us far less than the possibility that we might miss seeing Our Lady. We prayed all the way up to his house, asking her to wait for us, and she did.

Two thousand people were crowded around Mr. Januszkiewicz's back yard, where he had erected a large manger scene near his pool, and of course, the shrine he had built in honor of Our Lady.

The crowds were known to number more than ten thousand during the warmer summer months, and police officers were always on hand. Six portable toilets had also been installed on the property.

When Mr. Januszkiewicz came out from his house, he went over to the shrine. There was a large statue of Mary dressed in white alongside a large cross. Both were surrounded by bushes that people had adorned with yellow and white roses for Our Lady. Mr. Januszkiewicz stood in front of the statue and seemed to begin to pray. All of a sudden, he fell to his knees, and the crowd fell silent for the eight minutes or so that Our Lady was with us.

As people began to leave, for the most part still relatively hushed by the experience they had partaken in, my daughters and I decided to linger a bit. We wanted to have a closer look at the shrine itself. This became more difficult than we thought because we were going in the opposite direction of the crowd, so we stood to the right of the shrine to wait for most of the people to clear the way.

As we were standing there, another onlooker cried out that Our Lady had not left, that she was still there. The woman had been looking over the roof of a neighboring house when she saw the Blessed Virgin hovering near the treetops. The woman was weeping and speaking to Our Lady, partly in English and partly in another language, which someone told me was Filipino. Naturally, we looked in the direction she was pointing and, although I did not see Our Lady personally, we were all struck by an overwhelming scent of roses permeating the air.

My youngest daughter, Lisa, was a junior at Fordham University at the time, majoring in psychology and minoring in theology. As soon as she smelled the roses, she began to laugh and cry and tremble all at the same time. She was seeing Our Lady and described her as wearing a white dress, and on her head was a blue veil with a crown of coral-colored roses. Lisa said there were blue and white lights dancing around Our Lady's head, eclipsing everything around her, even the trees.

Mary Jo and I have visited other apparition sites, including Medjugorje and Conyers, Georgia. We both know without a doubt that Our Lady was truly appearing in Marlboro, New Jersey, as well.

My friend Dorothy, who was with us and who recently received a masters degree in art and teaches at two schools, also saw Our Lady's silhouette.

As wonderful as this experience was for us, it was Lisa's friend, Annette, who received a real gift from the Blessed Mother. A student at Fordham, too,

Annette had lost her mother two and a half years earlier, and the pain of her loss had not abated. She had been grieving and fighting a terrible depression all that time, but when Our Lady appeared that evening, she spoke directly to Annette: She told her that her mother was in heaven with her, and that she was watching over Annette. The young girl cried that night, but for the first time in almost three years, they were tears of joy. Now she is smiling again and enjoying life, which is exactly what Our Lady wishes for us all.

MARY V. LIMONGELLI
Hartsdale, New York

MARIE

PAUL AND I were married in May of 1988, and in September, his mother, Mary Ann, was diagnosed with a rare form of ovarian cancer. Paul was devastated, and with good reason. His father had died of a brain tumor when he was only three, and his mother had raised him and his three sisters and a brother all by herself, working as a coronary care nurse. Our families were very close, a true blessing that has given us strength time and again.

By 1989 Mary Ann was given a short time to live with no hope of recovery. Surgery and treatment had not helped at all. In fact, she soon was completely bedridden with an abdominal tumor so large that she looked as if she were pregnant. All of us knew that she was dying.

In the fall of 1989, Paul, a photographer and editor of television news, got a job at KDKA in Pittsburgh, where he met a fellow news photographer who had recently been to Medjugorje. He himself had experienced a miraculous healing, physically and spiritually, through the grace of the Blessed Mother. It was such a life-changing event for him that he was taking a group over to share the experience with others. When he heard about Paul's mother, he suggested we take her to Medjugorje to see if she could be healed through the intercession of the Blessed Mother.

Paul was all for it, while my reaction was: "Are you nuts? Let's just wait a minute here. I've never even been on a plane before and you want me to go where? Medja—what?" I kept saying, "Why do we have to drag her all the way to Yugoslavia? Can't the Blessed Mother hear us right here?" I was really very upset. We didn't have the money, either, but then Paul stepped in, and I'll let him relate what happened next.

PAUL

I REALLY WANTED Marie and me to do this for my mother, but I wanted her to feel right about it, too.

So I said to her, "This is like me saying I love you to you but then never doing anything for you or to support our marriage. We always say to God that we love him, but then we don't do anything for him. This is a way we can show him, and the Blessed Mother, that we have faith in them and that we care about them."

Marie was convinced after that, but then came my mother's doctors, who said, *"No way!"* They were sure she would never survive the trip. Frankly, I didn't know if she'd even last long enough to make the trip.

I had also lost my grandmother by this time, who I loved very much. She died at the age of ninety, but my mom had exactly the same look. The chemotherapy and the radiation treatments had ravaged her, and the tumor had attached itself to her liver and other abdominal organs. The cancer had also continued to spread throughout her body. She looked like she might not last another day, and then Marie and I really began to question what we were doing. If she died while we were away, we probably would not be able to make it back. In the end, my friend from work persuaded us to go for her and not to worry, that everything would be all right. And so early in 1990 we made the trip.

Each day we prayed for my mother, and on the third or fourth day, Marie and I began to feel this incredible grace enveloping us. It built up very quickly and so strongly that we felt as if we had stepped into the edge of heaven. We were overwhelmed with a sense of peace and purpose, so much so that we even decided briefly to stay and make a living for ourselves in Medjugorje! But then we realized that the Blessed Mother had something else in mind. A very special priest from a neighboring village made the whole point of people like Marie and me coming to Medjugorje very clear.

Father Jozo said something that has really stayed with us: "The reason the Blessed Mother wants people to come here, to Medjugorje, instead of her going throughout the world converting hearts, is very simple. She is doing it here because she needs to bring us out of our spiritually hostile environments into her own environment, where she can work on our hearts and then send us back out into the world. In the same way, you wouldn't ask a surgeon to come into your home to operate on you. It would be much too dangerous, so instead you go to his environment, which is much more conducive to successful healing." I guess we were not meant to stay!

MARIE

BY THE TIME we returned home, Mary Ann was not only alive, she was actually sitting up in bed, stronger than before we had left. On Good Friday in 1990, she went for a CAT scan, and no tumor could be found! The local hospital technicians were so baffled they thought their machines were faulty, so they sent her to another hospital to redo the test. There, a trace of the tumor was found, but it had shrunk ten times in size. The doctors took a whole battery of tests. They even brought in a specialist to match up her bone structure to make sure she was really the same person!

Shortly after the results of all these tests came back, Paul's mother was declared to be free of cancer. The doctors told us they could not call it a remission since it was so much more than that, and they had no way of scientifically explaining how a tumor of such mass could virtually vanish. But we knew that we had been to the edge of heaven, and we had opened our hearts, and the Blessed Mother had heard our prayers.

Mary Ann returned to work full time as a coronary care nurse, feeling absolutely fine and living without any medical treatment for a full year. She lived with joy and gratitude for the extra time she had been given.

Paul, Mary Ann, and I decided that we wanted to return to Medjugorje, this time to thank the Blessed Mother for her intercession. The trip was great, but on the plane back home, Mary Ann began to feel sick. We attributed it to the strenuous trip, but after a few days, she still did not get better. She went back to the hospital where it was discovered that her cancer had come back, this time to her colon. She had more surgery, as well as aggressive chemotherapy and radiation. She continued her treatments for almost two years, but in May of 1993, Mary Ann died.

She passed away at home, with everyone gathered together around her bed. We said to her, "Mom, you are going to a greater place where you are not going to be sick anymore. We're all going to miss you—but we love you very much, and we're really happy for you that your suffering is going to be over soon."

Mary Ann had loved her husband so much and really longed for him since he had died. Now she would have a chance to see him and be with him again.

It was terribly, awfully sad, but there was a definite peace about her death and that kind of peace can only be given by God. Paul's older brother, who lives in New York, was the only one who wasn't there when she died. He jumped on a plane as soon as he heard that her end was near, but he was two hours late. It was very hard for Paul to tell him that she had already gone, but we all believe she went straight to heaven!

This woman, Mary Ann, was so sick and she *never* complained! She never said a word about her cancer, and if you asked her how she was doing, she always smiled, said she was fine. She never got down. I know I'm going to sound biased, but Mary Ann Ruggieri was a lady of incredible grace and compassion. At her funeral, we had people, patients of hers from twenty years ago, come up and say, "You know, Mary Ann stayed up with me all night long and just held my hand!" She was really something!

Paul had made a promise to the Blessed Mother when Mary Ann was declared cancer-free that he would do something for her, but he didn't know what.

He decided to draw on his background in communications, speaking out at local schools against the violence in television programming and some rock videos that can negatively affect young people. We both believed that it was important to spread the Blessed Mother's word to young people, help educate them so that there would be a place in their futures for spiritual growth. Eventually, Paul even put together a little book called Answers for Troubled Times. It includes questions and answers about the true teachings of the church, and he now travels around the country speaking to young people everywhere.

The extra time Mary Ann had to enjoy her life on earth was definitely a blessing from God. That year brought Paul and me an entire lifetime of direction and purpose.

PAUL AND MARIE RUGGIERI
Pittsburgh, Pennsylvania

MY EXPERIENCES with the Blessed Mother throughout my life have been truly remarkable. What makes them special is that they not only gave me the gift of life, but taught me about death. That is the message I really wish to share.

Illness has been the catalyst that has brought the Blessed Mother to me. The first time occurred when I was nineteen. I had contracted polio, or more accurately, a strain of the polio virus. Back in the fifties, before the discovery of the Salk vaccine, anyone who came down with polio was thought to have come down with *polio*, but the medical fact is that there are many different levels of the virus. A friend of mine had contracted polio, and when I saw her husband on the street one day, I asked if we could go have coffee somewhere, which we did. Without being aware of it, this man must have been a carrier of the strain, because fourteen days later, I became deathly ill, had to be hospitalized, and was diagnosed with polio.

It was a very demanding time for me, my health so critical that it is hard to remember and describe all that happened during my illness. But one evening, a woman suddenly appeared, standing in the center of my room. She was breathtakingly beautiful, and behind her was a tunnel of light, like a narrow golden glow leading from her to somewhere beyond this room, this hospital. I wasn't at all frightened by the woman or the tunnel. As she moved to a far corner of the room, I remember thinking: "Who is this woman? She is the most beautiful person I have ever seen in my life." And I wondered why she was visiting me.

The next thing I knew, a nurse was standing over me taking my pulse, and I realized that I had obviously just been dreaming, and it was the nurse's presence in the room that had brought on my vision. I recovered fully from my bout with polio, and I didn't think another thing about the beautiful woman and the tunnel for several years.

Some time later, in 1978, my husband and I were vacationing in Mexico, where we did a lot of diving and swimming which we both enjoyed. Several of us who were at the same place came down with something that seemed like the flu. We were achy and uncomfortable and our throats were sore, but they all got better—I didn't. I continued to get sicker, and when I returned home to New York, my doctor insisted upon doing a spinal tap. He sent the spinal fluid to the Tropical Disease Center in Atlanta for analysis, and I continued to worsen, bad enough to be hospitalized.

My husband was deeply worried, and sat by my bedside day and night, watching over me, comforting me. And it was during one of these vigils that he saw I had stopped breathing. In a panic, he summoned the nurses and the doctor who came quickly, sticking me with needles, connecting me with monitors. My husband later told me all this because my only recollection, other than being very confused and disoriented by all the noise and activity, was of leaving. Leaving that bed, that room, that hospital.

I simply left all that noise and activity and panic and found myself in a dark room that was warm and comfortable and—*nice*. Out of the darkness, in a corner of the room, appeared this beautiful woman, and this time I knew I was seeing the Blessed Mother. Again that golden tunnel of brilliant light glowed behind her. I reached out to her and said, "If you would just come a little closer, I could take your hand and go with you." She was absolutely beautiful! She was wearing a long white robe with some gold embroidery on it. It's really so difficult to describe her kind of beauty. She was just someone you wanted to love immediately, and I did! I wanted to go with her so badly, but she answered, "No, Martha, you can't come with me now. You have work to do." Her voice was kind, but firm, and I knew that, as much as I wanted to be with her, she wouldn't let me go. I continued to travel back and forth several times between my hospital bed and that dark, peaceful room filled with the love of the Blessed Mother, but, of course, I eventually ended up in the room with the tubes and the needles.

The only two times in my life I had been seriously ill and both were caused by a strain of the polio virus— and both times I was visited by the Virgin Mary. I remained healthy for quite some time afterward, but when I did get sick again, it was very serious.

It happened in May of 1991. This time I was diagnosed with cancer of the colon. I was operated on immediately and the surgery revealed the cancer had spread from the colon into the abdomen and had invaded my lymphatic system. My doctor put me on a treatment consisting of thirty-five radiation sessions followed by chemotherapy. In November, after six months of this agonizing routine, I was retested and found to be clear of cancer.

By the grace of God, I had been healed. But my

doctor wanted to be sure that I wouldn't have a relapse, so he had me continue the chemotherapy.

My next set of tests were done in February 1992, and this time they showed results of a very different nature: the cancer had returned. My surgeon called a meeting with me and my family to tell us the devastating news. Because I had relapsed so quickly, and because the cancer seemed to be of such an aggressive nature, his prognosis for me was not good. He said that, statistically, I would not have more than one to two years left to live—at best.

My oncologist recommended continued chemotherapy for three months and then retesting to decide what further measures to take, like additional surgery. My family and I decided, however, to seek a second opinion. We went to a doctor at Cedars of Lebanon Hospital in Miami, Florida. He presented my case to a panel of his peers, and their expert medical opinion was to do nothing for a few months. Since I was relatively comfortable at the time, and since the prognosis was so bad, they didn't see that any real benefit would be gained by either surgery or continued chemotherapy at that time. I therefore opted to discontinue all treatment. That was February 15, 1992.

I had heard about Conyers, Georgia, where the Blessed Mother is said to appear to a woman named Nancy Fowler. My husband and I made the trip there, a journey that seemed particularly blessed to me under the circumstances—with the miracle of the sun washing the sky in orange, green, lavender, pink, just bursting with colors, and the extraordinary rainbow we saw as we drove, stretching from horizon to horizon like a ribbon of life.

One of the side effects I had been suffering since my initial surgery and radiation treatments was constant diarrhea and abdominal discomfort. Yet during our entire stay in Conyers I was fine—the minute we left, though, I was back looking for the nearest restroom.

But that certainly is not the highlight of my visit to Conyers! A priest who had heard about my condition told me about a nun there who prayed for terminally ill people. Sister Connie Galisino from St. Francis Hospital in Greenville, South Carolina, had been quite successful in her healing ministry. She made no claim—and no one made the claim for her—that she could always effect cures, but it was said that she could often bring a peace, an emotional harmony and healing to the dying and their families.

We arranged to meet with Connie shortly after we left the house where the apparitions of Our Lady took place. As she prayed over me, it was uncanny, really, but I immediately felt a rush of heat flow over my entire body, from my head, my face, down through my torso, to the tips of my toes. I began to tremble, and the next thing I was in that dark, quiet place of peace with a warm light in the center. Several minutes later, I opened my eyes to find myself lying in the grass. I had been unconscious.

I was desperately ill for two weeks after we returned home, but then, without any warning, I began changing—significant changes that left me feeling stronger and healthier. It was just ridiculous, but I began to feel lighter and lighter, as if an enormous weight had been lifted from me. By May 1, I felt and looked healthier than I had in years.

Of course, no one—not my friends, not my family, and certainly not my doctor—could believe my inexplicable improvement. On May 6, 1992, he told me the unbelievable news that my condition was reversing! A growth had disappeared; my lymph nodes were decreasing in size—and I felt great! Then, on July 31, he tested me again. This time the news defied medical science: I was free of cancer of the colon. Another test, this one on January 26, 1993, and my doctor declared that he was calling my condition not a remission, but a cure!

The doctors have no way of explaining how or why my cure happened, but I know. The Blessed Mother has always watched over me and I pray that she will continue to intercede in my healing so that I can help others by sharing what I have learned.

I know, from my terrible illnesses and from living with cancer, that death need not be feared. Perhaps this is why Mary has granted me more life, why she did not want me to go with her yet, and said that I had work to do here. My work is to let people know that they don't have to fear something that truly is beautiful. I wrote an article about my cancer and my faith for a newspaper here in Florida, and I speak at prayer groups and spiritual gatherings as often as I can. The Lord has been very good to me, putting me in touch with people who have cancer, specifically those who are just beginning, or finally at the end of, their journeys.

If my experiences and my faith can comfort others, I am delighted. I want people to know that life is glorious, but it's okay over there, too. And that next step is not frightening!

I hope people will learn how much easier it is to live, and let go, when you accept the beauty that lies waiting for us beyond this world.

MARTHA SEDLAR
Boca Raton, Florida

FAITH

At morn, at noon, at twilight dim,
Maria, thou hast heard my hymn:
In joy and woe, in good and ill,
Mother of God, be with me still.
When the hours flew brightly by,
And not a cloud obscured the sky,
My soul, lest it should truant be,
Thy grace did shine to thine and thee.
Now, when storms of fate o'ercast
Darkly my present and my past,
Let my future radiant shine
With sweet hopes of thee and thine.

EDGAR ALLAN POE

OUR LADY has had a really big impact on my life, and being in Medjugorje with her changed just about everything for me, from how I looked at life to my career.

In 1987 I went to Europe with my younger brother. I was about twenty-one at the time, and when we returned home, my aunt asked if we had been to Yugoslavia, which we hadn't. She had been hearing a lot about a place there called Medjugorje, and she gave me an interesting article about it. Although I had been raised to be really open to God, and I believed that apparitions were possible, this kind of thing just wasn't part of my life then.

The next year I went back to Europe with my older brother. We had worked like crazy during the school year, holding down two jobs and working weekends to save up enough money to backpack across Europe. Still, my brother could only stay for a month and had to go back, to work. We left each other in Ireland, and I decided to head for Turkey because I had heard you could buy good leather there at reasonable prices. I wanted a leather jacket, that was my sole motivation for going across Europe, to buy a jacket.

I wasn't very up on my geography, but when I pulled out a map, I realized that I would be going through Yugoslavia. I decided I should at least check out Medjugorje, but all I knew is that it was near Sarajevo. On the way, I had to change trains in Belgrade where I would have a two to three hour layover. I used that time to find out how to get to Medjugorje, but nobody knew anything about it, and it was hard to communicate because I didn't know the language. I ended up missing my connecting train, and getting more and more obsessed about finding the small, remote mountain village. I think the only reason I pursued it so much was because of the miracles I had read about. My attitude at that point was like, "This is going to be so cool. I'm going to see a miracle. Then I'm going to Turkey to get my leather jacket. When I get home, everyone will be impressed by my jacket and my miracles."

Eventually, I found a branch of an American car rental company. Assuming someone there would speak English, I went in and a man who happened to be turning in his car overheard—and understood—my questions. He, too, had heard about Medjugorje. He didn't know exactly where it was, but suggested I go to Mostar, which he knew was close. I went there by train, almost convinced that I was on a wild goose chase, but when we pulled into the station there were tour buses all over with Medjugorje stickers on them.

I made arrangements with one of the buses, and soon I was seeing the huge steeple of St. James Church. I was really excited, thinking, "This is it. This is where the miracles are going to happen. This is where my life is going to turn into one big, beautiful story."

Despite its remoteness, the village was teeming with people, many of them camping out in tents since lodging was not as abundant as it has become. I set up my tent next to an Irish family—a mother and her two daughters, who were about sixteen and ten. They were very welcoming, offering me some tea and telling me the schedule when everything happened. I asked if they had seen a miracle yet, which they hadn't, but they did know a lot about the history of Medjugorje. Excusing myself from information that bored me, I went to the church for the evening mass in English.

I was surprised by the multitudes of people present, until I learned that the apparition would take place at six forty. The visionaries were in the balcony, at the back of the church, where Our Lady would appear to them. At the designated time, I looked all over, but I never saw the Blessed Mother. Afterward, the mass continued, and as far as I was concerned, it seemed to go on forever. I went back to my tent, disillusioned and disappointed. I decided to give this place three days, three days for a miracle, then I was out of there.

My attitude didn't improve much the next day. I went to the two mountains with my camera, thinking that when my miracle happened, I was going to get it on film. At the service that evening, I was impressed by the number of people my age who were praying so devoutly. Yet I knew that this wasn't for me, and I decided they weren't my kind of crowd.

On the third day, I left the service early to go pack, since I was leaving on the eight o'clock bus the next morning. The Irish lady was surprised I was leaving so soon, and invited me to accompany her and her two daughters on a walk up one of the mountains.

It was an extremely dark night, and no sooner had we started walking than I began to feel really weird, almost uncontrollably weepy and emotional. As we neared the top, it got so bad that all I wanted to do was cry, but I told myself I couldn't do that because I was a guy, and guys don't cry in front of girls! I was holding back the tears with such an effort that I thought the rosary beads would break from squeezing them so hard. I felt totally out of control, and so uncool, but I couldn't help it: I couldn't hold back the tears a second longer.

Even as I was sobbing, I felt Mary envelop me in a mantle of peace. The intensity of her love was overwhelming. I felt so warm, and protected, and safe. Suddenly, everything in my life made sense—I now understood that the miracle I had been looking for was happening in that instant, inside of me. I had been brought here to learn that, and I felt so excited. It was like my life became an exclamation point!

I didn't leave the next morning. I spent the rest of my time in Europe in Medjugorje, which ended up being close to a month. My life was never again the same. The energy of that place became a part of me, and I wanted very much to become a part of it. I was a business major in school and had, until then, been making plans for a career in marketing, but suddenly I knew I had to do something with my life that was not just for my own gain. I began to reevaluate myself, my goals, where I was going, what I needed.

When I got home, I told my parents that I wanted to return to Medjugorje for Christmas, and I prayed every day to Our Lady to help me find a way to make it possible, financially. I believed I had a gift, but I didn't know what it was. I believed it had something to do with giving, and I needed to return to that place to learn more.

I started working yet another job to earn more money. Then one day, in September, one of my brothers spotted an envelope outside of our front door, with my name on it. There was no other writing, no postmark, only my name. I opened the envelope, and there was no letter either—but there was five hundred dollars in cash! I couldn't believe it. I asked everyone I knew if they had left it for me, and my mother asked every member of the family. Nobody knew where the money had come from. Our Lady had indeed answered my prayers, and I now had enough for my plane ticket to Yugoslavia.

My second trip to Medjugorje was very different. I had expected to pick up exactly where I had left off, on a high of excitement about finding meaning in my life. Instead, the first two weeks of my forty days there were spent in total depression. I felt a struggle going on inside me about whether to just quit and go back to my old life, or to take the next step in my spiritual development. I was sorely tempted to go back home, but I didn't. Instead, I started to pray constantly, and suddenly, one day, the depression was gone. I felt myself being lifted to a whole new level in my spirituality.

In the four times that I've been to Medjugorje, that second visit was the only time I felt challenged to give up. It was a pivotal point in my life, and it taught me to never give up hope. Not that anything really terrible was going on in my life, but it taught me he value of persevering, hanging in there with faith.

For me, Medjugorje is a slice of heaven on earth. It is a place that doesn't really exist in mundane reality, so the struggle is to maintain all the wondrous feelings you experience there when you are back in the real world, to keep the lessons in sight, instead of shelving them until your next spiritual journey.

I am a third year medical student now, and I am deeply inspired to practice this healing art. I have had to make an effort to find time for prayer. I lost that focus for a while when I started medical school. I was distracted all the time, studying all the time. Yet whenever I structure my day to allow time for prayer, Our Lady's arms are wide open, waiting to receive me.

I pray in the morning for the people I am going to meet that day. I see more patients now, and I pray that I will look in their eyes and see God.

I believe that we are all spiritual beings, but sometimes we let that part of ourselves go hungry. When we are given an opportunity to feed it, as I was in Medjugorje, it just blossoms and thrives because it loves to be nurtured. Our Lady has graced me with such an incredible gift, letting me experience the power of prayer. She tells us to pray for peace, and I believe that means pray for peace within our own hearts. If we have that, then we are able to love and accept other people for who they are, as Our Lady accepts each of us. Through prayer with her, I have been given the strength and confidence to dare to change, so that, hopefully, I can make a difference in this world.

TONY MADRID
La Mirada, California

I HAVE BEEN on a long, arduous journey since child-hood to find peace within myself. I grew up in a Jewish family that harbored some resentment toward Christianity, which is where I have been pulled. The inner conflict left me confused, and looking back on my life, I can't believe the level of bitterness, shame, even self-hatred that I once carried.

About twelve years ago, I began to see crosses everywhere. They would appear on my computer keyboard at work, on the road while I was driving, in my mind's eye as I fell asleep. Now, I had been meditating since about 1976, but these visions of crosses had never happened before. Having grown up Jewish, I was obviously confused, and a little dis-turbed by these images, so I went to see a rabbi about it. He very wisely suggested that it was prob-ably a sign that I was neglecting my spiritual life—which was definitely true.

I then started to take classes in spirituality, to try to understand what I was feeling. I also began to have mystical dreams which left me with the sense that there was a special presence in my life. This was both a frightening and an exhilarating sensation because it made me aware of how empty I had been inside.

The classes I was taking were at John F. Kennedy University, in the Graduate School of

Consciousness Studies, and they were very intensely oriented toward personal growth. This was such an enlightening period for me because everyone had their own spiritual practice at the school—it could be Buddhism or yoga or meditation, it didn't matter as long as you felt comfortable with it. I discovered that I had a real path with Christianity, and in particular, Catholicism. I shouldn't have been surprised by this revelation, given how I felt growing up and given the images of the crosses, but still, it was wonderful to feel the rightness of this path, and it's been the passion of my life ever since.

In 1990 I decided to make a pilgrimage to Europe to see a number of sacred sites, to get more in touch with my new faith, and so I made plans to be away for about four and a half months. I visited Lourdes and La Salette, and also several sacred shrines such as the one of the Black Madonna in a small town outside of Zurich. It was a very powerful trip for me, as well as one that brought me a kind of peace I had never known before. Medjugorje was particularly special.

I had been traveling alone, and when I arrived at Medjugorje I felt really lonely. I just craved companionship, someone to be with and share experiences with. Medjugorje is so small that there's no official bus station. You're dropped off at the side of the road and then you walk the two kilometers into town. Well, as I began to do so I met up with a guy I recognized from seeing at another site a few weeks back. We had gotten friendly then, and now here he was again, providing the companionship I so needed.

He was traveling with his girlfriend, and one night the three of us stayed up late, just sitting outside, looking at the stars in the night sky. It is a very remote area, and we could see like a million shooting stars! Then all of a sudden, the stars seemed to align themselves like a crown with three perfect circles next to each other, so similar to pictures of Mary's halo that I have at home. All around the triple crown were the shooting stars, dancing and sparkling, and it was very mystical to see.

Another evening we decided to walk up to the Hill of Apparitions, after hearing that Mary had told one of the visionaries she would be appearing at eleven o'clock that night. There were probably close to a thousand people there, and it was surprisingly quiet for so many people. Suddenly, there were flashes of light everywhere, just a blaze of light here and there, around, up and all over! It lasted for only a minute, but we all felt that the explosion of radiance was like an announcement that Mary had been there, bringing us her peace and love.

Whenever I feel lonely or afraid, I pray to the Virgin Mary. For me, she is the perfect Mother, never judging, always comforting. I have pictures of the Holy Mother all over my room at home and on my desk at work, and whenever I need her, I can just look at an icon or picture and I can feel her come to me, enveloping me in her love. Mary is the Mother who has never left me, who has never ridiculed me, never shamed me. She is always there and helps me in every area of my life.

Mary even guides me in my relationships. A woman at work recently asked me what I was looking for in a relationship, wanting to fix me up, and I told her that I need to be with someone who is as deeply committed to her spirituality as I am to mine. I want someone to go to church with, do rituals with. I will not compromise my love for God, or Mary, by accepting anything less than a spiritual union—even if that means staying single.

Spirituality has become the focus of my life. I meditate two hours a day, I read different scriptures, and I take classes, particularly in Christian mysticism. The more I learn, the more impassioned I become. For as long as I can remember, no matter how painful the circumstances of my life at the time, I always felt, even if it was only as big as a grain of sand, something calling me, giving me strength and hope. I can hear an inner voice saying something like, "Come higher. Come to me. Come closer. I am with you always," and I am comforted. This passion, this yearning for God is my life. It's like a heartburn that never goes away because the calling is so strong.

I don't know what your beliefs are about reincarnation, but I think it explains my passion. I had a regression with a therapist that was very real for me. I was told that I had been a priest or a monk in a former incarnation. And when I was in Assisi, I must admit it felt oddly familiar, like I had been there before. I've studied the early church in some detail, and I understand there was a Catholic scholar, Origen, who believed in reincarnation as well. The church may have feared that people wouldn't believe they needed salvation through the clergy, so it was written out of Christian teachings in 465. We'll never know if this happened for sure, but my experience with reincarnation is that it's true—but I certainly honor your beliefs if they are different.

My belief in reincarnation in no way diminishes my love for Catholicism. I love to go to mass and there is a great feeling of spirit and peace for me in the whole Catholic tradition.

For too long, I had been a rather bitter and depressed person, and extremely self-absorbed, filled with resentment toward other people. *A Course in Miracles* has really helped me get through this, showing me that my path in this lifetime is union with God. In order to achieve that, I had to make changes. I started by changing jobs—going from negotiating multimillion dollar deals in the defense industry to working with a behavioral health care firm. And now I pray for other people instead of trying to preach to them. It is by leading my life with the spirituality that is so important to me that I have come to shed the bitterness and resentment, and most important, reach outside myself to help others gain greater faith and understanding.

My faith was dramatically put to the test about five days after I finished graduate school. I had been out for the evening, and when I returned at about eleven o'clock, I found that my house had burned to the ground. Apparently my roommate at the time had been barbecuing and the fire marshall thought that an animal, smelling the traces of food on the grill, knocked it over. The old wood house we lived in caught fire and I lost everything I owned. I didn't even have a toothbrush left!

I called my parents on the East Coast, and they were, understandably, very worried. Without even really believing what I was saying, I told them, "Don't worry. It's all going to work out." As soon as the words were out of my mouth, calm and peace of mind settled over me, and I knew that everything would be fine. No one who knew me then can believe this attitude when I tell them the story because I usually worried about everything!

It turned out things were more than fine! People came out of the woodwork to help me. People I didn't even know were giving me things—people I didn't even like. I got clothes, stereos, cameras, color televisions, even kitchen appliances that I didn't even know how to use, like a wok, a crock pot, and a waffle iron. The Salvation Army was there for me, as was the Red Cross, even my parents! I knew that the presence that had once been no bigger than a grain of sand came through for me the night of that fire, and will remain with me forever.

It is said that the hardest journey is from the head to the heart. For years I have intellectually understood all that I have studied of God, but it is only recently that I am allowing myself to make that journey to the heart. Mary has done that for me. She has given me the experience of *feeling* her divine presence actively at work in my life. She has made me see that God is really working for me. That's when spiritual yearning—questing—becomes what Mary wishes for us all: faith.

SCOTT SHNURMAN
Concord, California

I WAS BORN in Texas, to Mexican parents. I'm married to a country girl from Tennessee and we have nine children, six grandchildren.

I have worked in radio and television all my life. During my forty-five years in communications, I met all the movie stars you could think of when I worked on *The Mike Douglas Show*. I was at the NBC station in Philadelphia, channel 3. I was often asked to speak at schools, to elementary children up to high school kids. I always accepted and went so that I could get all the students excited about their lives and discover what to do with their God-given talents.

In 1981 something extraordinary happened. I was invited by the company I worked for to speak at a Texas University. This time I was to motivate and excite students about pursuing careers in science, math, space, robotics, computers, etc. When I finished my twenty-five minute talk, the dean of engineering and other professors came running up to me, saying I had touched them. Some felt that I had been speaking to them personally, that I had answered questions they had about their lives, their faith. They invited me back to speak to the teaching staff. Again I accepted, and more people felt that they had been touched spiritually by my words.

Then letters began to arrive from the students. Many of them expressed a desire to do great things with their lives. Some of these same students also shared their feelings of inadequacy in life and how they had seriously been considering taking their own lives. Now, they wanted to live.

I questioned why these changes were taking place in others when I would speak. I never knew what was going to come out, and I wondered what they were hearing. I prayed and asked God for answers.

In 1987 I received my answer, but not the way I expected. One day as I was getting ready to leave for work, I tripped coming down the stairs from the second floor. When I hit the bottom step, I had fractured my sacrum and coccyx bones. The doctors told me bluntly that I would remain in pain and would be able to walk only with painful effort unless an operation was performed. And for the next four months, I was in great agony. Desperate, I finally gave in, asking Mary and Jesus for help. The Holy

Spirit came through. The message was clear: I had offended one of God's children.

"Who are his children?" I kept asking myself. "We all are," I kept answering. So I started with my own family. No answer there. I jumped to my work at the TV station, where I had several hundred people under my supervision. Still no answer. I then went on a mental worldwide trip, searching the recesses of my mind for friends I might have offended. I hit California and bingo! I could not believe it, but I saw I had hurt some friends of mine. Without hesitation, I picked up the telephone and said, "Before you hang up, I'm calling to ask forgiveness. I must have been a fool and I'm sorry." I cried, they cried. We prayed and they, in turn, asked me to forgive them. After two hours on the phone, I hung up feeling excited and happy. I felt free.

I decided to thank God in a special way. I wanted to do it on my knees. But how? I couldn't move one millimeter without screaming. I was alone at home. And once on my knees, I could never get up without someone helping me. I always had two telephones in case I needed help. But again, I repeat that I had to thank God on my knees.

I decided to roll sideways from my bed and fall to the floor. And that's when it happened. I will describe it the way I experienced it and still remember it clearly today. First, I thought an earthquake had hit. My body went up in the air and I was thrown about three feet away from the bed. I was then dropped right on my tailbone. I yelled for help. I was really scared.

When I hit the floor, two things came quickly to mind. Even if the tailbone had not been broken before, I felt it was completely shattered now! My next concern was how to get up and back on the bed. I was alone in the house, and I needed help. I stretched my right arm toward the bed to see if I could drag myself closer to it. I did this very slowly because it was going to hurt—but as I reached out, I didn't feel anything. What was happening? I lifted my entire body from the floor by pushing down with both hands, and again, nothing hurt. It was mystifying! I went for the final test. I reached under my body and slowly pressed on my tailbone. And now I was really shaking because there was no pain.

I started talking to God, looking up to the ceiling. "Is this supposed to be a miracle?" And I heard a voice in my room. "Why don't you get up and walk?" Strangely, that voice didn't scare me. I answered back, "It better not hurt!"

I got up and couldn't believe it! I kept jumping up and down like a kid, saying "I don't believe it! I don't believe it!" Then I ran up and down the stairs, the very stairs that I had fallen down. I kept saying to myself that miracles do happen, but not today. Two thousand years ago, maybe, but not today, and especially not to me. I went down on my knees easily, without pain, thanking the Blessed Mother and everyone I could think of in heaven.

I went downstairs, fixed a fresh pot of coffee, and waited for my wife and daughter to come home. They nearly fainted when they saw me in the kitchen, with my feet up on the table. I was smiling happily, drinking my coffee. I told them exactly what happened, and it was my daughter who said, "You were touched by the Holy Spirit." I had no idea what that meant, but she continued. "You better ask God what it means. Maybe he has a plan for you, Dad!"

I went to the doctor and the X rays showed no cracks anywhere in the coccyx or sacrum bones. My wife and I vowed to pray for thirty days in gratefulness for what had happened, and to find out why. The first of many answers came when I was invited to speak at a convention of employees from a major airline in Los Angeles.

During dinner, I related the miraculous healing of my tailbone to the west coast manager. As he listened to my story, his eyes widened. He blurted out, "I think you came here for another reason. God sent you to help my sister!" When I asked him what was wrong with her, he told me that she had been a teacher in Germany. She had been sent home, to die, because of ovarian cancer that was spreading rapidly. She had only about thirty days left to live. He wanted me to see her. I refused. I certainly wasn't a healer and I didn't want to get their hopes up. I just didn't want to have anything to do with her. He pleaded, begged, almost cried. "She is thirty-three years old and I don't want her to die!"

"What will I say? What will I do?" He yelled back, "Why don't you let God tell you what to do and say." Finally, after four hours and forty cups of coffee, the waitress threatened to throw us out. I gave in and went to see her.

I said things I never, ever would have dreamed of saying, things I couldn't make up. I put her through a three-point plan when I didn't even know what the three-point plan was! As I talked to her, I began to see what her problem was. She absolutely refused to forgive her ex-husband. She also hated her oldest daughter, because she looked like him. I told her bluntly that she had no choice. She still refused to forgive him. I also told her that the hatred she had for her daughter was manifesting itself on everyone that surrounded her, including herself. "If you don't start loving and forgiving everyone, that hatred is going to kill you before the cancerous tumor that you are carrying around!"

I got up to leave, assuring her I would be back in thirty days. She asked me what I was coming back for, and I said, "For your funeral. Out of respect for your brother and family, I will be back for your funeral. You are going to die, you know?" Then I added, "Do you know who is going to cry the loudest at your funeral? *Me!* Last night I rejected you for four hours in a restaurant. I didn't even want to see you!"

She looked shocked, and I continued, adding, "Why can't you accept something that God is telling me to tell you? You have no choice. You have to forgive your ex-husband."

She finally broke down. She cried and hugged me, asking if forgiveness was really possible. "Of course it is," I assured her. "It's not easy, but we have no choice. Jesus' first words from the cross were, 'Father, forgive them, for they know not what they do,' and look what he went through!" Then I asked her, "Why are you letting your ex-husband hang on to your neck, torturing you? Why don't you turn him over to God? If you really believe he deserves to be punished, let God take care of it!"

She cried again. We prayed together and I told her that for the next thirty days not to pray for the healing of her cancer, but to pray for the healing of her soul. To ask God to give her the strength and guidance to be able to forgive. And she did. And the cancer disappeared. She was shocked—and so was I! Eight years later, she is still teaching, in Germany again, and I have gone there to speak to the American servicemen as well.

When I returned home, I told my wife everything that happened. We prayed again, for answers, for guidance. And we both got the same answer:

I was operations manager at the TV station. I was running it night and day, making lots of money. I don't know what lots of money is, really, but I was making over a hundred thousand dollars a year, with benefits on top of that. I could eat out in restaurants. I could rent cars, helicopters, planes, whenever I wanted to. I could come and go as I pleased—but I could no longer serve two masters. Either I stayed at the television station, making money, serving man, or I give my life to God and serve him. Three weeks later, I terminated my own employment and gave my life to God.

That incident was eight years ago now, and I have never wanted for anything. It propelled me to a "ministry" which I still refuse to call as such. If anything, my ministry is a simple one of love—sharing love—God's love. And it begins by loving and forgiving everyone.

I have been all over the world, to Ireland five times, and to England, Puerto Rico, Mexico, and all across the United States. I'm available the year round to anyone who wants me. If someone calls, I'll come. I have so much love and compassion for people, and all I want from life is to be able to help everyone God puts in my path. I want others to open their hearts and minds to be and feel free—that they may never again be afraid to love. That's when miracles begin and never end.

I see so many people struggling and suffering, people who have lost their faith. I have also seen so many miracles happen when we let God help us. Everyone kept telling me I should write a book about the spiritually hungry people of the world who are always looking for answers, but usually in the wrong places. In 1992, I did just that. It is called *Another Kind of Hunger*, and in this book, I share a series of miracles that God allowed me to witness and be a part of.

When I look back at my life today, I see that whatever happened in all these years, whatever prompted me to write my book, it was all made worthwhile by what happened to this one married couple: A woman called me from Germany last year to tell me that her marriage had become turbulent and desperate. After years of hatred between her and her husband, she decided to kill him, and then kill herself. Then someone in Texas mailed her a copy of my book. She couldn't put it down. She asked her husband to read it, too. They chose to forgive each other and are now at peace. She only called to share their experience, and to thank me for writing the book.

Don't we all deserve a shot at forgiveness, a chance to live, and love, again?

Tony Zuniga
Penndel, Pennsylvania

I guess it would be fair to say that awareness of faith began for me in the third grade at the St. Joseph's Junior Military Academy, but I had no idea then, nor for some time after, that the Blessed Mother was preparing me for something special. Still, I know now, looking back, that the foundation I received from the third grade carried me through the turbulent sixties, the political seventies, the greedy eighties. That foundation also was with me through a variety of career changes, including doing a tour of duty for the U.S. Army and serving as an undercover narcotics agent for the South Carolina Law Enforcement Division. I've also worked for a mental health facility, and then after a few years of this and that, I went to the University of Pittsburgh for graduate school before finally deciding to return to the family business, which was seventy-five years of funeral directing.

As the years went on, and as I got older, I developed a callousness, a cynicism toward lots of things, including God and church and the Blessed Mother. Oddly, though, despite this attitude, I would always find myself back in church on March 25, my birthday, I guess just to say thank you for being given another year. Eventually I learned that March 25 is the feast day of the Annunciation, when the Angel Gabriel appeared to the Blessed Virgin and the Word became flesh.

Now, on my forty-first birthday, March 25, 1989, I woke up really dissatisfied with my life. My marriage was not particularly fulfilling, my life in general left me restless; in short, I was having a midlife crisis, but unlike most people who question their jobs or their family life, my crisis was spiritual. I was wondering what it would be like to give the next forty years of my life to God, and then I thought how presumptuous that was of me. After all, who said I'd even have another forty years! But that morning I acknowledged to my cynical self that it was only by the grace of God that I had even been given this day. And that's when the process of divine renewal began in my life, a daily journey that leaves me amazed at what God is willing to do for me since I truly gave my life to him.

On Good Friday of that same year, 1989, a reported miracle happened at Holy Trinity Church. The eyes closed on a crucifix suspended high up near the ceiling. There was a lot of media commotion about the event and I felt there was something special about this incident that pulled me to see it for myself. My wife, Nikki, had no interest in taking the drive out with me, but my two children, Ryan and Julie, accompanied me. It was a Thursday and they were off school for Easter break. I still remember that after I parked and we were walking into the church, an elderly man was leaving. His expression was beatific, I don't know how else to describe it, and that's when I knew for sure that something remarkable had to be happening here.

My children had never been inside a Catholic church, so I explained about the altar and the tabernacle, the various statues and holy pictures. We went up to the altar and kneeled, and this incredible feeling washed over me, warming and comforting me, and without even thinking about what I was doing, I reached out to bring my children closer to me and then my eyes started to well up with tears as this tremendous emotional wave crested in me. It was just awesome.

We went back to our pew, and after a few minutes, we started to leave. At the door, I asked Ryan, a precocious six year old at the time, if he was ready to leave. He looked me steady in the eyes, and said, "Dad, are *you* ready to leave?" My son understood me better than I understood myself, because I *wasn't* ready to leave, and so we spent some more time there, the first step on my path back to God.

The next several days were devoted to private contemplation as I tried to sort through the maelstrom of emotions I was experiencing. I ended up talking with a friend I trusted completely, telling her what had happened to me at that church. She suggested I speak with her hairdresser, who had been to a little village in Yugoslavia. She felt that he could be helpful.

My wife was in utter shock when I visited this man and she could see that I was actually considering going over to this unpronounceable village in a strange country. I am black; I had married into the black Baptist Church where I was a trustee and a golfing buddy of the pastor. Why would I be interested in the Catholic church, in phenomena regarding the Blessed Mother? My success in the funeral business depended upon my association with the black church—what in the world was I thinking of? she wanted to know. What I was thinking of was how much longer could I prostitute myself by going to church only for the sake of my business.

It was clear to me that I needed something to fill the spiritual void I felt within, but how? I began to pray for clarity and guidance, and I received it from one of the hairdresser's clients who ran the Pittsburgh Center for Peace. There was a trip planned to Medjugorje in June. My mother had planned to go to

China at the same time, and I didn't know if we could both be away from the business at the same time, but I decided to go ahead and take the June trip.

"You can go anywhere you want and do anything you need to do," Nikki said to me when I told her, "if you think it's going to help you get your life together. But whatever you do, Toby, do it quick, because I might not be around much longer." And upsetting as this was to hear, I wasn't surprised by her feelings. My remoteness had not helped an already fragile marital situation that I still wanted saved.

The next day I wrote out the check for the trip, and as I did, this wonderful sense of peace came over me, a feeling that everything was finally going to be okay. It was like 'no deposit, no return'—and writing that check was the biggest deposit I would ever make in my spiritual life. Ironically, that same night was when the riots in Tiananmen Square broke out, and my mother's trip to China was canceled. I felt that the Blessed Mother was really making it easy for me to return to God.

On the very day I was to leave, though, I couldn't find my passport to save my life. Naturally, I was frantic, just tearing the house apart. I knew I was going to miss my flight and then what? If I couldn't go on this trip, I really didn't know how I could go on—that's how much I had invested in it emotionally. I got down on my knees and prayed to the Blessed Mother for her help. If she would only help me find my passport, I prayed, I promised to make changes in my life she'd be proud of. I don't think it was even two minutes later that I went out to the car, and there on the front seat was my passport! I like to think that since then I've kept up my end of the bargain!

I was the only black person in a group of one hundred and one people, and I knew absolutely not a soul. But at the airport I noticed one man in a golf shirt, and I figured that would at least be a good conversational gambit. It turned out that he was an attorney also traveling alone to try to sort out his life—and we had been slated as roommates!

That first evening we took a walk up the Hill of Apparitions, and before we left, our group leader suggested we pick up some stones to take with us in remembrance of the holy ground. I took four or five, put them in a small, leather pouch I had, and placed them under my pillow before I went to sleep that night.

On the third day, I woke up at about 6:45 A.M. with an image of what I can only describe as a television screen in front of me. There was a pathway and on the right, a large boulder; on the left a figure wearing a brown monk's robe tied at the waist was hunched over. Then this figure started to shuffle toward the rock. As it bent down, hands folded in prayer, it looked at me three times and then the center of the pathway unfurled.

I saw these little people on a ladder that was coming out of the ground in ascendance toward heaven. These little people just kept coming and coming. The praying figure kept looking at me and I didn't know what any of it meant. "Blessed Mother, what are you trying to tell me?" I prayed. And then she appeared briefly on this vision screen, as if to confirm that I was not hallucinating, before she quickly disappeared again.

When my roommate woke I told him about my vision, what I called MTV, for Mary Television. He didn't have a clue as to its meaning either. After lunch I decided to climb Mount Krizevek where the huge cement cross is, thinking that maybe that was the pathway up the mountain I had seen and I would find my answers up there. By the third station of the Cross, we were all hot and thirsty, and we stopped for a drink of water when one woman lost her equilibrium and fell, hitting her head on a rock. We didn't know whether to continue or not, but then we noticed that this particular station represented the time Christ fell carrying his cross up the hill at Calvary. When the fallen woman heard this, she was determined to continue, which we did.

When we got back down, our group leader was there waiting. He had gone to church instead of making the climb with us. He was very excited. "You'll never guess what happened to me," he said. "I was praying in church when I saw these little people, dressed in gold, coming down a ladder from heaven!" I then told him I had had the same vision, except that in mine, all the people were going up the ladder! "This place is awesome," I said out loud. "What an awesome place to be!"

The next morning, before I got out of bed, I whispered, "Blessed Mother, what is on my agenda for today?" She appeared to me in a corner of the room, in a pale blue veil and a darker blue garment that seemed to billow about her as if there were a breeze. She answered my question audibly, by saying: "Pray." And believe me, that's what I promised to do all that day. Then she made a left turn and drifted out through the wall.

I think I must have lost six or seven pounds of water weight during my time in Medjugorje—crying out all the garbage in my soul and leaving it there. I never felt so good in all my life!

Upon my return home, I bought a new bible, and after flipping through it briefly, I found a passage, Genesis 28:12, about Jacob's dream of a stairway to heaven: "A stairway rested on the ground with its top reaching to the heavens and God's messengers were going up and down on it."

How true it is that anything we need to know can be found in scripture. "Seek and ye shall find; ask and it shall be given unto you."

I read more about Jacob, how he had come to a sacred shrine and fallen asleep on a stone—and I had put the stones under my pillow the night before I experienced my vision. Jacob dreamed about God's messengers, exactly the same image I had had. I read further how Jacob had exclaimed, "Truly, Lord, how awesome is this shrine!" There was that word, awesome, again, and as I read, I found myself welling up with emotion.

I returned to Medjugorje to thank the Blessed Mother for all she had shown me. My wife even agreed to have our marriage blessed in the church so I could receive the sacraments.

For me, life has become an exquisite new banquet of joy. I have been led to a consecration to the Blessed Mother, to study the role of angels, to accept the guidance of the Holy Spirit. Seeking to fill the spiritual emptiness that brought me to Medjugorje also brought me to God's warehouse, where all you have to do is pull up your spiritual wheelbarrow and fill it up with as many graces as you can handle at any one time.

We have been given so many gifts—wisdom, understanding, counsel, piety, knowledge, fortitude—and all we have to do is ask Mary for them, appreciate them, and use them. She is there for us, all the time. That is the key, understanding the divine presence. Our Lady is using this time as one of grace and preparation for our enlightenment. Each rosary bead is like a little drop of oil for our lamp. Each time we touch one of the beads as we pray, a drop of oil falls into our lamp, and the more oil we have, the brighter our lamp will glow to illuminate the path for somebody who is in darkness. I understand that now, as I also understand the true meaning of living in faith, extending the love we feel for God toward others.

I have learned about letting go of pride and ego in exchange for the love and charity that the Blessed Mother has to offer us. This is a holy surrender that brings more than one can ever imagine.

And I have learned that peace comes from having love in my family once again. The Blessed Mother is here with us to share her messages of hope, love, and joy. I pray I may be able to do so the rest of my life.

May God bless each and every one of you.

TOBY GAINES
Evans City, Pennsylvania

MONICA

OUR WHOLE life has dramatically changed in the past twelve years. My husband, Stephan, is French and worked as a professional musician. I am Jamaican, and at the time the events began to happen to us, I had been working as a fashion model. We were living in Europe, spending most of our time with a circle of friends who were anything but spiritual. Everything changed once we visited Egypt, and after our first visit, we would return time and again, often living there for periods up to six months.

I'm no longer a model. Instead, I write about religious icons, researching, recording, and documenting information. Stephan has become a master of the art of Coptic Christian icon painting. He is one of only three masters alive in the world today. He trained under Dr. Isaac Fanous in Cairo and took his Ph.D. at the Royal College of Art in

London. He has exhibited his work in London and Jamaica, and spent two years adorning Coptic churches in Los Angeles. Stephan now lectures at the Visual Islamic and Traditional Arts Department in London, and I think he can best describe the journey of faith that we have taken.

STEPHAN

IN 1982, AFTER Monica and I had been married about five years and were living in London, we were booked to go to the Caribbean, where I had a recording to do in Nassau. For some reason we changed our minds, and we now believe that we were led to go to Egypt instead.

We went as a spiritual pilgrimage. I particularly wanted Monica to go to Zeitun, where the Virgin Mary had appeared some ten years earlier. Monica suffers from a blood disease known as sickle-cell anemia, and it is pretty devastating when an attack strikes. In Egypt, she was feeling fine, and I was the one who got sick while visiting a very important monastery in the middle of the desert called Al Maharakh. The Holy Family stayed there for six months and ten days. The altar is a stone, a monolith, where the family lived and it is on that very stone that the Christ child was dressed and tended to. It was a very special place, but it was also where I caught typhoid and very nearly died.

I was so sick that I began to vomit blood and had to be taken back to Cairo, where I was well enough to leave for Alexandria. There, however, I promptly fell ill again so it was back to Cairo. A friend there insisted we go to church, but the first two we stopped at had already started their services. The third church was packed, but at least we were in time for communion. I was so sick, I was afraid I was going to vomit right there. I sat down, my head throbbing, and it felt like there was a forest of people around me. I could hardly stand up because I hadn't eaten for so long and I really wasn't supposed to take communion, because we are Orthodox. When it was time for us to go up and receive the sacrament, I was literally carried along in the throng of people. The instant I received the holy sacrament, in that microsecond I was healed. When we left the church, I was balanced, I was walking, I was well—and I was ravenous. We bought some holy bread, the first solid food I'd had in two weeks. I've not suffered since then.

Monica and I were in Egypt for one month on that first trip, and prophetically, it was the same month when the Fast of the Virgin is celebrated. The day after my healing, I met Dr. Isaac Fanous, the man who was to become my master in the study of iconography. We had admired his work at the Coptic Center in Cairo, not knowing who he was or where he was from. Ironically, this man that I was to study with for the next ten years lived only three doors from the home we were staying in. That trip was the beginning of my life as a sacred artist, and I thank the Virgin because I believe she called us there to Egypt.

As Monica has said, we were to return to Egypt

time and time again over the next ten years. We traveled all over the country, visiting the monasteries and places the Virgin had been during her flight into Egypt. Our lives completely changed.

One of my favorite icons that I do is the Virgin of the Sign. According to the prophecy of Isaiah, a Virgin shall conceive and bear a child, and that child shall be Emmanuel. The sign is that the Virgin shall bear, and I have come to believe that she is the Virgin for this modern day. It is a contemporary image of her, which I feel best expresses what we are all experiencing with her. The Virgin carries us, her children, in her bosom.

Monica and I always feel carried, protected by her. Even in the worst of circumstances, she helps. Although we sometimes have to go through bad experiences, like getting seriously ill, and you feel like you are at the edge of the abyss, the Virgin is there to keep us from falling in.

In 1989 we were in Jamaica when we read in the newspapers a story of a lady who claimed that the Virgin wanted to bless a certain spot in the Blue Mountains, which happens to be where Monica was born. The Virgin wanted this land dedicated to her, and in return would bestow many graces and healings to the people of Jamaica.

Now in Jamaica a very popular custom is afternoon tea parties. These are very fashionable affairs, and are often very political, with the wives of the ministers hostessing. It is not unusual for a tea-leaf reader to be invited as entertainment. A party such as this was being given in Miami for eminent Jamaicans and the tea-leaf reader who had been invited fell sick, so another lady was asked. This second reader was said to have had dealings with Nancy Reagan, and had accurately predicted the blowing up of the Challenger and the coming of Hurricane Gilbert that had swept the island in 1988. It was this lady who was being written about in the newspapers, as having had a vision of the land the Virgin wanted dedicated to her. The reader's description was very detailed: she saw a mist covering the land, with white flowers everywhere. There were two palm trees and a spring, where it was said that the Virgin would bless the waters, so that the people who came would be healed.

Soon after the tea party, a man got in touch with the reader and said that he was willing to donate a piece of land he had in the Blue Mountains if a chapel were built there. There was a lot of uproar about this because Jamaicans are predominantly a Protestant society and rejected the idea of having a sanctuary for the Virgin Mary.

Monica and I happened to meet the sister of the man who owned the land and we went up to see it on the morning of October 31. You could feel it was a sacred place the moment you stepped foot on it. It was absolutely breathtaking! The smell alone told us the Virgin was there. Roses are traditionally associated with her, but so, too, are the white ginger lilies that abound in the Blue Mountains. As we were walking, we saw the mist as the tea-leaf reader had described, and we saw the white lilies in bloom everywhere, and we saw the two palm trees. The man who owned the land insisted that there were three trees on the property, but then he discovered that Hurricane Gilbert had broken one, so the reader was correct about that, too! There was a spring as well, which the owner hadn't even known about. Everything just sparkled with an amazing feminine energy, the energy of nature at its ripest.

The issue of the land and the Virgin quieted down for a while, and we didn't hear any more about it until 1990, when we were on a plane from London to spend six months in Jamaica. We were sitting next to two Jamaican ladies who were returning from Medjugorje, and just raving about their experiences there. We began to speak about the Virgin Mary, asking them whatever happened to the Virgin of the Blue Mountains. They told us that the Jamaican family in Miami had paid for a white marble statue of the Virgin to be made in Italy to sit on the land, but it never made it there, and nobody really knew why.

According to the tea-leaf reader's vision, the Virgin had foretold of negative things happening to Jamaica if her presence was not recognized. The island turned her away as she tried to bring the people back to a more spiritual way of life, and the result has been a marked increase in crime and violence, especially amongst the youth. The island is also being desecrated, as trees are being razed everywhere for profit.

Yet it is said that where evil abounds, grace is there also. Despite the troubles the island has suffered, Monica and I feel very close to this country. We want to settle there. We have even found a place we really love, an eighteenth century stone house that needs a lot of restoration, but we know it is right for us. It's in the parish of St. Mary, in an area called Highgate, and the house itself has a meaningful name: Hopewell! So these are all symbols of the Virgin— from the high gates of Zion to the well of hope, also known as the Fountain of Life. They speak to us and assure us that the Virgin has once again led us home.

STEPHAN AND MONICA RENE
London, England

WHENEVER I speak of my experiences with Our Lady and Jesus, I feel it is very important for me to begin by honoring my parents, who are remarkable people. They have ten children. They trusted in God that He would always provide for us. My mother once said that whenever she was going to have another baby, my father would get a better job or somehow we were able to afford the new arrival and added expense. When I think of the daily sacrifices they made to raise us, I am amazed. I know their faithful example greatly influenced the person I have become. So, my relationship with God is based on a solid Catholic faith handed down to me from my parents.

I was on a retreat in high school when I began to learn more about the truth of what my faith proclaimed. I began to pray and read scripture that increased my understanding of God. Then when I went to college, I stopped practicing my faith for about five years. I let other ideas influence me. Finally I realized that something very important was missing from my life, and I set new goals. The first goal was to establish a daily time for prayer. I began once again to pray and read scripture. With the devotion that I gave my new prayer life, I began to have interior images or visions.

The first time I saw Mary and Jesus in one of these images was in 1987, while I was praying. My eyes were closed, but I could see them in front of me. I stretched out my arms to praise them, and then Jesus, standing on my left, took my hand. Mary, standing on my right, took my other hand. What seemed to be an electric current of love ran through my body. It was incredible. I had the knowledge that they were uniting with me, protecting me, and pleading to God for the forgiveness of my offenses. My past had displeased God, so they were explaining to Him that they would help me become a better person and faithful servant. The sensation was overwhelming. It was a complete and perfect understanding of love.

I continued to pray and study scripture while working a full-time job and volunteering at church. Within a few years, I was given a job as youth director for a church. During that time I met a woman named Theresa Lopez, who was allegedly seeing apparitions of Mary. I had the opportunity to witness some of these apparitions at her side. We would go to the Mother Cabrini Shrine in Colorado to pray. Another woman named Veronica Garcia and I soon began to see Mary, too. The three of us eventually also began to see Jesus and many other saints and angels.

Mary and Jesus continually reveal themselves and the reasons why they are intervening in our lives. For the purpose of this book, I will share with you some of what I have seen and heard.

First of all, Mary and Jesus have a great love for us. No matter what offense we may have committed, they still want us to come to them so that we can begin to grow and learn about them and ultimately experience God's love for us through them.

Mary needs our prayers. She once appeared to me standing illuminated in an abyss of darkness. She was suspended above a large black thorn bush. The thorns were six to eight inches long. I could see the hem of her gown tangled in the thorns. She was unable to move as the thorns grew thicker and closer to her feet. She said, "Sing . . . sing . . . sing!" I began to sing to her. As I sang, a cushion of air developed between her hem and the bush. She was freed from the thorns and began to move closer to me. She said, "The world offers me thorns, but you offer me a way to the world through your prayers."

Why does Mary need to come into the world? Why is she appearing to so many people in so many places? I asked her those questions. She did not hesitate to communicate with me about the answers. She has made it clear to me that the purpose of her coming to the world today is the same as it was over two thousand years ago when the angel, Gabriel, announced to her that she was chosen to be the mother of God's Son. Her role then was to bear Christ into the world. In scripture Mary said, "Let it be done unto me according to thy word." This "yes" was not a singular "yes" but rather a perpetual "yes." Today her obligation is the same: to bring Jesus the Savior into the world. It is her duty to bring Christ to God's people so that during every generation, Jesus can be born in the hearts of His people. Now, in this moment, she comes to present her Son to us. She appears in so many places, for it is her duty.

Mary has illustrated for me why, in this century, she comes so often. She allowed me to see a desert. Then I saw a drop of rain as it fell to the desert floor. The drop immediately evaporated once it hit the hot sand. Then the Blessed Mother said, "If God wanted to make the desert bloom, He would not send a single raindrop." This message helped me to realize that Mary is like the raindrop. She began initial appearances at Lourdes and Fatima, not unlike the first drops of rain that fall in the desert when spring begins. Since then reports of apparitions of her have come in a deluge. This outpouring of communication points to the spiritual crisis of the world. People are wandering about in the dryness of an unquenched spirituality. God desires his people to flourish in understanding and love of Him. Therefore, He has allowed Mary, the mother of His Son, Jesus, to repeatedly and overwhelmingly reveal herself to us. Through her apparitions and messages, we are drenched with an awareness of God that enables us to have a deeper knowledge of Him, thus allowing our spirituality to blossom into a vibrant relationship with Him.

Her visitations to various places throughout the world have helped me to understand that she is intervening in specific ways for different cultures. These cultures are often isolated from the world due to a lack of modern technology and media. Therefore, people do not always have access to the necessary books and educational tools they need to discover God. Also, even if these areas have access to the appropriate means, the people do not always use them because the traditions have been lost or altogether halted by influences of government, lack of popularity, or simple apathy. Mary comes to revive fervor and faith. Skepticism often squelches reports of apparitions, and the revelations are not allowed to be spread. So Mary simply moves to another region and begins her work again.

The nuances, customs, and traditions vary greatly, for example, between Betania in Venezuela and Denver, Colorado. Try to imagine sending a cancer specialist to treat people suffering from malnutrition in a poverty stricken area. The cancer specialist could help, but would most likely be less effective than the doctor who specialized in malnutrition. Jesus has been called the "Great Physician" and He knows what needs to be done in order for a particular region to be restored to spiritual health. That is why God allows Mary to appear in the form of native people. Mary does not want to be intrusive, rather she desires to be inclusive for the people she is visiting. She comes in the most common manner for the greatest understanding and consolation, thus she can be the most effective wherever she is.

The Blessed Mother is always thinking of her children's well being. She also intervenes because of the breakdown of our emotional and psychological existence. In America, we often lead such separate lives. Loneliness plagues this country. God did not intend for us to live in isolation. We were created to live together in harmony and peace. Through her apparitions and messages, Mary is telling us that God loves us. She asks us to live in peace, especially in the messages she gives to Medjugorje.

Before the Industrial Revolution, we lived in a more communal family setting. We had the support of extended families. We had aunts and uncles, grandparents, neighbors—a community to give us stability—and a solid foundation of mentors to guide us. Today we are often separated from our natural parents, grandparents, and family members by the demands of modern living. Being mobile for employment, and the time demands placed on us by everyday activities, leave us little time to spend with one another. More and more of our time is spent less and less with the people who could be our spiritual mentors. It has become the exception, not the rule, to associate with our immediate family and neighbors.

Mary and Jesus are very close to each other and they want us to be close to them and one another. At one point I was allowed to see inside their home. It was very simple, with white plaster walls and carved wood beams and shutters of a deep brown hue. It was enchanting. Mary was sitting at a heavy wooden table with a gold chalice and plate sitting in the middle, as if on an altar. Jesus was standing in the doorway. I could feel the immense love that they have for each other and the "family of man." They are available to everyone regardless of race, color, or creed. They don't care about the amount of money a person has, or the size of the house a person lives in, or the make and model of the car a person drives. They never judge us by our mistakes or the lack of understanding we have of God. They have the desire to help you understand your life, why things happen for the reasons that they do, and how your life can make a difference for God and others.

Another lesson Mary taught me has to do with inspiration as a means of communication. I was talking to a priest about my visitations and messages from Mary and Jesus when he mentioned that he had never seen or heard Mary, but he often felt inspired.

Later that evening the Blessed Mother told me to go to the father and tell him, "I would prefer to use inspiration as a means of communication because it allows you to exercise your faith to the greatest capacity, and it allows me to remain completely humble." This message helped to remind me that an act of faith helps to strengthen our relationship with God. I told the priest the next morning after mass what Mary had said. I believe Mary would want everyone to know what she said, too.

Mary and Jesus are continually revealing themselves in many ways. We have the Bible, the Pope, priests, religious family members, friends, books, radio, television, and so many other forms of communication, but because we often don't get the information we need to understand God and our faith, Mary and Jesus intervene.

God loves us so much. He wants to see us thrive. God has a great need for us to unite against the atrocities of evil. You can help Him through your prayers and works of charity toward one another. I will continue to pray for you and your needs, and I urge you to do the same for yourselves, as well as others.

Please make time to pray! Prayer is an embrace. It is the time you go to God to meet and speak with Him. During prayer God will help you understand Him and His unconditional love. No matter what happens, you can always be sure of God's love for you.

SYLVIA L. GROEGER
Littleton, Colorado

A FINAL NOTE

I say that we are wound
With mercy round and round
As if with air: the same
Is Mary, more by name.
She, wild web, wondrous robe,
Mantles the guilty globe,
Since God has let dispense
Her prayers his providence:
Nay, more than almoner,
The sweet alms' self is her
And men are meant to share
Her life as life does air.

GERARD MANLEY HOPKINS

IN THE COURSE of writing *Gifts of Grace*, I heard a story about a woman who was vacationing in Europe. She was a rather well-known writer and speaker, and decided to spend an afternoon sitting quietly in one of Italy's magnificent cathedrals. In the middle of her prayers and meditations, she lifted her head and was very startled to see Mary appear before her, especially since she is not Catholic. She looked left and right, then behind her to see if anyone else was aware of what was happening. When she found a nun sitting behind her, she thought she understood. She returned her attention to Mary saying, "I think you have the wrong person. I think you're looking for her!"

I love that story and I think her feelings might be shared by many. No one really knows why Mary comes to them, but come she does, even though there is no discernible pattern amongst those she chooses to visit. There is no common denominator between us, but once Mary has graced us, we share the indisputable fact that our lives are altered by her presence.

The stories in *Gifts of Grace* are by, and about, ordinary people of all faiths who were blessed by a divine presence. What, then, do we consider divine? To Catholics and non-Catholics alike, it is the power of love above all else. Mary knows God's love, and she brings that love to humanity. She melts our hearts, allowing us to see the world differently. She inspires us to extend the love we feel from her to others, to share our joy.

Mary is the embodiment of what our society has lacked, or negated, for so long, namely a gentle, feminine strength, full of grace and compassion.

As we head toward the millennium; as we see countries torn apart by civil strife; as we hear ceaselessly of man's inhumanity to one another, we must ask ourselves if change is possible. We have become engulfed by fear, of sickness and poverty, of violence, and perhaps even worse, indifference. Can the world be delivered from this fear? *Yes.*

Mary is here to do just that.

She is here to awaken our sleeping hearts, to take the scales from our eyes. We are not morally dead, just numb; not blind to others' pain and misfortune, just too scared to look. She is here to strengthen us, giving us the gift of her graces, promising us a vision of—and a path to—a more loving world.

Mary knows what is possible for humanity, but she is willing to start with one person at a time. I hope this book has convinced you of that.

Some people have already been touched by her. Others are about to be called. But what Mary wants us to remember is that we don't have to wait for her to come to us. We can go to her daily—in prayer, in meditation, and in devotion. We can light candles, set aside time for her in our lives, and learn to talk to her as if she were, truly, present to hear us. I know she is waiting for us, and she is the one person who will never turn us away. Her arms are always open, reaching out to us.

She has an answer for every problem or difficulty that we will ever experience; a balm for every wound.

Mary has a promise to fulfill, and that is to lead us back to God. As she told one of the visionaries in Medjugorje: "I have come to tell the world that

God exists. He is the fullness of life, and to enjoy this fullness and obtain peace, you must return to God."

For more than two thousand years, the Virgin Mary has gifted us with her graces. She is here for us all. And she will not leave until we are, once again, united in the peace and love of God.

ACKNOWLEDGMENTS

There are many people who have helped and encouraged me. I would especially like to thank:

Al Lowman and B. G. Dilworth, for being the agents I hoped and prayed for.

Diane Reverand and Trena Keating, for their gracious support.

Susanne Jaffe, whose words infused this book with the feeling it deserves.

Karen Goldman, for introducing me to Authors and Artists Group.

Bawa Jain, for helping me remember our time with Mary.

David Cerf, for all those years, for the friendship still.

Christine Barber, for the fun we've had, for watching me grow.

Sandi Bailey, for still being there.

Chip Fichtner, for so many things he doesn't even know he taught me.

Paxton and Anne Robey, for consistently refusing to believe in my drama.

Cynthia Stibolt, for her faith, belief, and trust.

Kristi Pamperin, my omnipotent oracle of knowledge.

Sandy Ingerman, for helping me to find my soul.
Robert Zimmer, for giving me my first opportunity to write professionally.
Don Meehan, for selflessly making so many introductions.
Larry and Barbie Dossey, for their kindness and generosity.

Shaun Jensen, my brilliant brother, and my friend.
Kenny Jensen, for his independent strength.
My parents, Erling and Lillian, who brought me this far.

Most of all, I would like to thank everyone who shared their stories with me,
and Mary, for bringing us together.